THE HISTORY OF
IPSWICH

THE HISTORY OF
IPSWICH

CAROL TWINCH

First published in Great Britain in 2008 by
The Breedon Books Publishing Company Limited
Breedon House, 3 The Parker Centre,
Derby, DE21 4SZ.

This paperback edition published in Great Britain in 2013 by DB Publishing,
an imprint of JMD Media Ltd

A catalogue record for this book is available from the British Library.

ISBN: 978-1-78091-363-6

Printed and bound in the UK by Copytech (UK) Ltd Peterborough

CONTENTS

INTRODUCTION

The success of Ipswich as a settlement has relied in no small measure on its geography – the freshwater springs from the hills round about, the shelter of a river estuary and proximity to the open sea and the wider world beyond. Since Neolithic times and before, all the requirements for human habitation were there: water, wood and other means whereby to subsist, trade and prosper. But these very advantages at first proved also to be its curse. Positioned on the east coast of England, it was vulnerable to the incursions of invaders from mainland Europe, and the River Orwell that served its trade so well was an open invitation firstly to the Angles and Saxons and then to Viking warships that brought marauding adventurers who all but razed it to the ground. Yet it survived then, and again early in the 11th century when William the Conqueror almost destroyed it in anger. The story of how Ipswich survived to become one of the longest-inhabited towns in England is the subject of this book.

Although Ipswich is not named in documents until the 10th century, archaeology proves that it was established almost 400 years earlier. It was the first town to be founded in Suffolk and Norfolk, and was the capital of the eastern Angles (East Anglia). Before the astounding discoveries made at the Sutton Hoo burial site in the 1930s little was known about the East Angles, which perhaps accounts for the fact that the story of Ipswich does not feature more prominently in the history books. The connection between Sutton Hoo and Ipswich was not made immediately, but the patronage of the Wuffinga kings provides answers to many questions as to the origins of Ipswich.

Since it is obvious that such an enormous catalogue of political milestones, personalities and customs over two millennia is unlikely to fit in a single volume, *The History of Ipswich* aims only to outline how the town got to where it is today. It traces events with a broad brush from

Neolithic times to the present day, though aficionados of the town annals might rue the omission of familiars from the role call. Yet even a book with three times as many pages would not tell the whole story of the granting of King John's Charter, the political and religious implications of mediaeval times and the story of wealth creation and intellectual life in Elizabethan, Georgian and Edwardian times.

The town has made friends along the way, most especially in America. Many of the 17th-century settlers who set sail for the New World came from Ipswich, and the 'occupation' of about 80,000 American servicemen and women in Suffolk during World War Two could not fail to leave enduring links. American personnel continued to be stationed in Suffolk during the Cold War and only in the 1990s did they begin winding down their operations. There is a steady stream of genealogical enquiry passing to and fro across the Atlantic as the descendants of those who left these shores in the 17th and 18th centuries attempt to find their roots.

Ipswich has lent its name to four towns in the United States of America (the most famous being Ipswich, Massachusetts), one in Jamaica and one in Australia. The Queensland Ipswich was a penal colony at Moreton Bay, the first convicts arriving in 1825. The town was originally called Limestone, after the mining industry there, but in 1843 it became known as Ipswich. The name change was proposed in honour of the Governor of New South Wales, Sir George Gipps, apparently because of the 'Gipes' in Gipeswic, the Anglo-Saxon name for Ipswich.

Since 1993 there has been a special relationship with Arras in Pas de Calais in the north of France. In 2003 a new Charter of Co-operation was signed, the two communities agreeing to co-operate on the mutual objective of promoting education, economic development and cultural, sporting and social exchanges.

For help along the way, thanks are extended to the Blue Guides, who do sterling work in promoting Ipswich history, and to Brian Dyes

(Ipswich Transport Museum), Chris Elmy (Lockdales), the late Russell Fellowes, David Kightley (Ipswich Numismatic Society), Keith Wade (Archaeological Service Manager, Suffolk County Council), Colchester and Ipswich Museum Service, and the staff at Christchurch Mansion.

CHAPTER ONE

EARLY GIPESWIC

There is no doubt that there were people living in and around prehistoric Ipswich. Archaeological evidence shows that man has lived here since at least 5,000BC. Neolithic axes have been found near the town site, and in 1968 five gold Iron Age torcs were found during construction work at Belstead. A sixth torc was found nearby about a year later. All six are in the British Museum and constitute one of their two most famous collections of first-century gold torcs. Scientific analysis shows that they are made from a mixture of 90 per cent gold and 10 per cent silver, an alloy that helps to establish that they were made around 75BC. They were worn around the neck and are made by twisting two rods of gold with the ends, the 'terminals', being cast on to the twisted rod. It is clear that those who made them had not only the skill to create them but also the capacity to enjoy such sophisticated and beautiful objects, indicative of a society not of savages but intelligent craftsmen.

To further establish human habitation in these parts, an Iron Age beaker was found at Brantham, and a collared urn, from a cremation burial at Rushmere, dates from the Bronze Age. Other important and significant finds have since come to light, leaving historians in no doubt as to the antiquity of settlement in the vicinity of what was to become Ipswich.

It might be thought disappointing, therefore, that the Romans made comparatively little of the place, although by the end of their tenure there must already have been the nucleus of a town, though not with any formal design. This is because the Roman invasion came north from Kent to make camp at *Camulodunum* (present-day Colchester) on the banks of the River Colne. Here they encountered the native Trinovantes tribe, which capitulated to the invaders soon after its king was killed in battle. When the legions reached what is now Suffolk they found a long-established and strong political geography dominated by the Iceni tribe, who proved a greater challenge to their authority than the Trinovantes. These were not primitive people, as evidenced by their coins and jewellery, although they were the descendants of the hunter-gatherers who had colonized the land after the last Ice Age. Men and women from the Icenian settlements around what is now Ipswich joined forces with their queen, Boudicca, in the winter of AD60 as she made her final and ultimately unsuccessful stand against the Romans. Proof of this came as recently as 2004, when a collection of rare Roman artefacts of international significance was found at Holbrook. They have been dated to around AD61, and in 2007 they were acquired by the Borough Council for exhibition at Ipswich Museum. Part of the find comprises the first complete set of Roman cavalry decorations ever found in Britain, looted from Colchester and buried at Holbrook by the retreating tribesmen.

Some disaffected Trinovantes had joined the indignant Iceni rabble, but after initially sacking *Camulodunum* they were defeated by the hastily assembled Roman legions and Queen Boudicca was killed. The insurrection failed and those Iceni who returned from the fight were a vanquished force. So began the Roman occupation of Britain that was to last over 400 years.

To date, the most important Roman site in Ipswich is at Castle Hill (Whitton) where a large villa was built in the second century. Excavations during the 1850s revealed a mosaic pavement and an amphora, indicating that the occupants were prosperous and the property was possibly an outpost of the new ruling hierarchy. Brooches, pins and gaming pieces were found, and later work carried out in the 1940s confirmed painted plaster on internal walls and a bathhouse that showed those living there to have been of some standing. They worshipped Attis, a life-death-rebirth deity and the lover of Cybele, a deification of the Earth Mother who had been venerated since Neolithic times. A festival was held in honour of Cybele on 25 March each year when there was feasting and rejoicing for the mother of the gods.

A mile away from Castle Hill, in Dales Road, a Roman cemetery was found to contain burials accompanied by grave goods consisting of earthenware pots and glass vessels, provided to sustain the dead on their journey to the underworld. Six of the skeletons had been ritually decapitated, the skulls being placed between the knees (one of which is on display at the High Street Museum).

Generally the Roman sites in and around Ipswich point to there being groups of smallholdings, ranging in size from small farmsteads to larger agricultural estates, rather than to a conurbation of any size. Remains of small farms have been found at Albany, Foxhall and Braziers Wood. Another holding at Chantry was occupied throughout the Roman period and a single Roman coin was found in the St Mary Quay area.

Within the modern town boundary there is evidence of isolated cremation burials in Carr Street, London Road and Burlington Road. In 1899 a large fourth-century burial was excavated along Tuddenham Road and found to contain 70 skeletons, some in lead coffins.

By the middle of the fifth century, the Roman occupation had run its course. By about 430 there had already been piratical incursions from mainland Europe, which the thinly-spread legions were less and less able to contain. Troops were gradually withdrawn to bolster Rome's own defences and other adventurous causes closer to home, leaving Britain to its own devices. Without the Roman legions to protect it, Britain was vulnerable to invasion and it was inevitable that before long there were new arrivals, although they would be of a different hue to those who had just quit. They were the Angles and Saxons (from what is now Germany and Holland) who began their colonisation of eastern England in about 450.

Just as the Romans had colonised the Iceni settlements, so the Anglo-Saxons moved onto land abandoned by the Romans and built a number of small hamlets along the Gipping and Orwell rivers. Ipswich – or Gipeswic, as it became known – was one of the first of any size to be founded and one of the earliest to be populated. Stoke was the shallowest part of the river and therefore the most easily bridged, and it formed the nucleus for what was to be continuous settlement in that precise location, which is what gives Ipswich its claim to being one of the oldest towns in England.

This time the invasion was almost imperceptible. There were no battles and the Anglo-Saxons did not bring an army with them. Instead they came with a desire for peaceful colonisation and to set up as farmers, craftsmen and traders, which they did with apparently little opposition from the Romano-British inhabitants. The seventh-century chronicler, Bede, writes that 'the Angles or Saxons came to Britain at the invitation of the king' and were granted lands on condition that they protected the country. They brought other languages, too, and for the first time in its history Ipswich had a name. Discussion is to be had over the precise origins of the name Gipeswic but the consensus is that it derives from the Saxon word *wic* (settlement) on the Gipping. Alternatively it was a settlement named for a leader called Gipe, or Gipp, though there is no evidence for either theory. By the middle of the 16th century it appears as Gippeswiche.

The two counties Suffolk and Norfolk took their titles from the South Folk and the North Folk, just as the Angles in the east inspired East Anglia. Gipeswic was one of the earliest of the new 'English' towns and has maintained constant habitation from at least 450 to the present day.

The precise form that Ipswich took at this stage in its history is a matter for conjecture and archaeology. There is no documentary evidence to refer to but there is sure and certain proof of its existence as a centre for trade and, therefore, formal urbanisation from at least 620

– which indicates that there would have been some kind of emerging town by the end of the sixth century. Much rests on ongoing research, the study of place names and, most importantly, contemporary 'finds' or ancient earthworks.

The earliest fragment of trade evidence is the type of pottery made in Ipswich from 625 until around 850 (Middle Saxon), now appropriately named Ipswich Ware. The centre of the potters' quarter was today's Carr Street with more kilns at St Helen's Street and Turret Lane. It is thought that there had been pottery workshops in Gipeswic since the departure of the Romans in the fifth century, but Ipswich Ware produced in the seventh century is not only distinctive but a unique type of mass-produced greyware, if dull and a little uninspiring. It is known to have been made on a hand-turned 'slow wheel' and differs from the faster 'kick wheel' used by the Romans. Gipeswic was the only place in England making this type of wheel-thrown kiln-fired ware, thus making finds of Ipswich Ware useful in assessing the contemporary trading area. Not only has Ipswich Ware been found all over Eastern England, the Midlands, Yorkshire and Kent, but also across Western Europe, an indication of the continuing links the new settlers had with their homelands.

The county's urban archaeologists have plotted find spots within Middle Saxon Gipeswic itself to conclude that it was some 50 hectares in size, 'fifty times bigger than the average rural settlement at that time'. Between 680 and 700 a massive and deliberate expansion took place. The new migrants revitalised an existing industry and developed a thriving export business that complemented other occupations, such as fishing, weaving, silver, leather and metal working. Evidence of significant trading of goods (with the Rhineland, Belgium and Holland) gives Gipeswic the indisputable right to claim unbroken trade from the end of the Roman era to modern times. Considerable amounts of wine were imported, and wine barrels originating in the Rhineland were re-used to line wells in the town.

Longship Screens by Anthony Robinson (1995), showing the Sutton Hoo helmet.

By around AD550 East Anglia had emerged as a new united kingdom and its ruling kings were called the Wuffingas. Very little was known about them and until the 1930s there were few, if any, connections made between Gipeswic and their Great Hall at Rendlesham. However, in

1930 the discovery of a seventh-century ship burial of unprecedented importance at nearby Sutton Hoo turned Anglo-Saxon history on its head and provided a possible reason for the success of the emerging Gipeswic. The internationally famous burial ground, four miles upstream from Woodbridge on the River Deben, was found to contain grave goods so rich as to befit only a ruler or king, immediately disproving historic assumptions about the people and culture of the time. These were not untutored barbarians. The figure was buried wearing clothes that glittered with jewelled gold and he had about him rare objects of beauty from the Mediterranean such as to express imperial and ancestral power. Urban archaeologist Keith Wade writes unequivocally of the royal house 'importing luxury goods, wine, fine garments, furs, slaves, etc., and distributing them among the aristocracy of their Kingdom in return for allegiance'. This suggests that Gipeswic was founded to control the economy, although the extent and nature of this early development is constantly being written and revised.

The most likely candidate for the Sutton Hoo burial is the warrior king of the Wuffingas, Raedwald, who died around 625. The king and his retinue at Rendlesham would have needed a port to service the many needs of the royal household for both trade and travel, and this would provide a perfectly respectable reason for the deliberate expansion of Gipeswic. What better than the River Orwell and an established, thriving settlement through which to conduct business? For its part, Gipeswic could only benefit from royal patronage, and attention of this sort must wholly have improved the status of the inhabitants. But what is the evidence for Gipeswic having been founded by the Wuffingas? It is, perforce, circumstantial, but nevertheless financial support from a rich royal could explain why the town prospered when many others failed. It was unlikely that the population could have financed the expansion from the potteries and fishing economy but management from the Wuffingas would have provided the confidence to establish a port of some

St Mildred's Chapel (left of the Market Cross) was built around 700 (Colchester and Ipswich Museum Service).

significance. Examples of Ipswich Ware pottery were found in the burial chamber, perhaps to show their patronage of a profitable industry.

The building of the Chapel of St Mildred on Cornhill in around 700 is one of the first manifestations of the urbanisation process and signifies the real start of the town. It is also one of the first outward signs of Christianity in Gipeswic and the dedication is likely to be one chosen by the Wuffinga kings. St Mildred died around the time the chapel was built and it stood alongside a hall thought to belong to the Wuffinga kings. It was Raedwald's son, Sigebert (c.630–40), who bridged the gap between paganism and the new religion. The Cornhill was purposely created as a central market and was the town's meeting place, then and now. St Mildred was one of the most popular saints in mediaeval England. She was a princess, being a daughter of the king of Mercia, and friend of the mother of Aldwulf, another East Anglian king. Saints of the very early church often belonged to the royal houses and the naming of the Cornhill Chapel is taken as another indication of the influence of the

Wuffingas. While most of the population were peasant farmers or relatively uneducated tradespeople, the political power remained firmly in the hands of the few and it was they who were instrumental in establishing Christianity. The chapel remained in use until the 14th century, when it was converted into the first town hall, and its outline appears on the first town seal of 1200.

Another link with the Wuffingas and the early history of Christian Gipeswic is the Liberty of St Etheldreda. A liberty was a collection of manors or other areas outside the jurisdiction of the sheriff. That of St Etheldreda, also known as Wicklow, consisted of a large section of east Suffolk, including most of Gipeswic. King Edgar granted the liberty to Ely Abbey in 970. Princess, saint and abbess Etheldreda was a daughter of Anna (c.640–54), another of the Wuffinga kings, who founded the magnificent Ely Cathedral and who, like Mildred, was among the most popular of the Anglo-Saxon saints. The Liberty of St Etheldreda survived until 1899.

It is not the role of history to speculate on what might have happened, but it is tempting to wonder how the Wuffinga dynasty would have evolved and what Ipswich would have become had ninth-century Suffolk not been ravaged and mutilated by invaders more ferocious than the Romans, and without the good intentions of the Angles and Saxons. The very words 'Viking raids' are enough to bring to mind the devastation that these marauding adventurers wrought on a peaceful, industrious East Anglia. The East Anglian martyr king, St Edmund (died 869) was unable to stop the bloody incursions, and the capitulation of his kingdom was swift. Much of East Anglia was ruled under Danelaw – 'the place where people lived under the Danes' law'. Although Ipswich was taken back into English control in 918, it was eventually to succumb again.

It is possible that Gipeswic was one of the places where the new Danish rule was fiercely rejected. It had, by now, a political structure and there is no reason to suppose the new order was either welcomed or accepted. In what is described as the 'second wave' of Viking invasion, presumably to mop up those recalcitrant areas that were still outside their control, Ipswich suffered two major Viking raids in the battle for supremacy between the Angles and the Danes. In 990 and 993, Gipeswic was attacked and burnt. Seven years later, in 1010, Thurkill the Tall captured Gipeswic for the Danish king, Cnut, and 'laid all waste'. In 1016 Cnut himself consolidated Gipeswic under the charge of Thurkill.

Whatever the nature of the town's defences, and it is thought that construction of ramparts across the north of the town was started by the Wuffingas in the seventh century, they were useless against an enemy approaching from the river. They were built to form the northern boundary of the town rather than as a defensive measure for the south. A town site 12 miles up-river was ideal for trading purposes but it was no obstacle for the Viking warships. By 1016 it was all over and, like all England, Gipeswic came under the rule of Cnut, king of England, Denmark and Sweden from 1016–1035, who for the next few years, ironically, gave the kingdom a period of peace and prosperity.

It is some consolation to the vanquished, perhaps, that the Danes left little in the way of memorials in Gipeswic and it retained not only many of its old traditions and customs but also its Anglo-Saxon name. Only the word 'Thingstead', the Danish name for a public meeting place, survived to the 19th century, when it was renamed St Margaret's Green. Cnut, though, left a more indelible legacy in the form of silver pennies minted at Gipeswic that bore his image and which are still turned up by metal detectorists to this day.

After 1016 the town gradually settled down and people got on with their everyday lives with less fear of constant disruption. Its ability to withstand violent change would seem to derive from the confident roots put down in the days of the Wuffingas. Edgar (reigned 959–975), who was king of all England in between the two Danish invasions, appears to have been disposed kindly towards it. He conferred the revenues of the

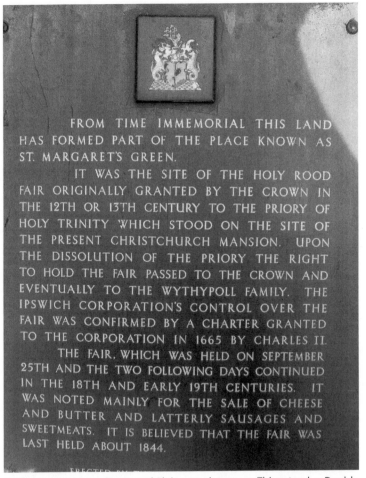

FROM TIME IMMEMORIAL THIS LAND HAS FORMED PART OF THE PLACE KNOWN AS ST. MARGARET'S GREEN.

IT WAS THE SITE OF THE HOLY ROOD FAIR ORIGINALLY GRANTED BY THE CROWN IN THE 12TH OR 13TH CENTURY TO THE PRIORY OF HOLY TRINITY WHICH STOOD ON THE SITE OF THE PRESENT CHRISTCHURCH MANSION. UPON THE DISSOLUTION OF THE PRIORY THE RIGHT TO HOLD THE FAIR PASSED TO THE CROWN AND EVENTUALLY TO THE WYTHYPOLL FAMILY. THE IPSWICH CORPORATION'S CONTROL OVER THE FAIR WAS CONFIRMED BY A CHARTER GRANTED TO THE CORPORATION IN 1665 BY CHARLES II.

THE FAIR, WHICH WAS HELD ON SEPTEMBER 25TH AND THE TWO FOLLOWING DAYS CONTINUED IN THE 18TH AND EARLY 19TH CENTURIES. IT WAS NOTED MAINLY FOR THE SALE OF CHEESE AND BUTTER AND LATTERLY SAUSAGES AND SWEETMEATS. IT IS BELIEVED THAT THE FAIR WAS LAST HELD ABOUT 1844.

St Margaret's Green, Street and Plain were known as Thingstead, a Danish name for meeting place.

Liberty of St Etheldreda on Ely Abbey in 950 (where the word 'Gipeswic' appears for the first time) and he maintained and improved the local mint, which went a long way towards ensuring the enduring status of Gipeswic (about which more in Chapter Two). Trade flourished

The Museum has a permanent exhibition, *The Ipswich Story*, charting 13,000 years of life in and around the town.

between northern France and the Rhinelands, and remains of several of the elite, probably merchants and traders from those countries, have been found in the Anglo-Saxon burial grounds, identifiable from their clothing and, often, grave goods. Society became more organised: laws were codified and there were written property deeds. The feudal system began to develop, whereby society was divided between the rich landowners (the church, king and lords) and the mass of the population, who carried on working and trading in relative but universal poverty.

The Danes, like those before them, took over the existing infrastructure, exploiting its advantages for themselves, and so Gipeswic survived and continued on its way.

CHAPTER TWO

NORMANS AND VIKINGS

By the start of the 11th century, Ipswich had a complicated and potentially sophisticated political and social structure. As Lilian Redstone points out, 'the traders and husbandmen owed duties to this lord or that, and paid to Queen Edith and to Earl Gyrth the royal rent of honey and fifteen pounds in cash'. Some men owed services to the lord of East Bergholt in addition to other divisions of rent and revenue, such as King Edgar's gift of Stoke to the monks of Ely. Christianity had put down roots and was an increasingly important part of everyday life, with 12 churches founded.

Those in trade, fishing or farming usually owed allegiance to someone, in one form or other, and the freemen continued to plough and harvest their land on the hills in the immediate vicinity of the town. There were mills at Stoke Hamlet, the ancient and lowest possible river crossing of the Orwell, at least as early as 1086. This provided access to markets south of the town. Already, Gipeswic had a convoluted past, a respectable amount of history and good prospects for the future.

It is still, however, a wonder that Gipeswic survived the next onslaught. Barely was life back on an even keel after the Viking invasions when along came the next wave of attack, this time from Normandy. Nothing was ever the same again. The Normans created yet another new ruling class, sweeping away much of the old English aristocracy and Anglo-Saxon traditions.

Unfortunately, the people of Gipeswic are thought to have mortally offended the new ruler, William I (reigned 1066–87), who took his revenge on them for their non-compliance and 'wasted' the town. Why he should have done so is not entirely clear, but the legend goes that it had something to do with Earl Gyrth of the East Angles, who led the Suffolk men at the Battle of Hastings (when four-fifths of the Ipswich burgesses were killed on the battlefield). The Earl's arrow had slain Duke William's favourite horse from under him and in retaliation, it is said, the Normans destroyed Ipswich. It is possible, however, that there were other, unknown political motives. Earl Gyrth was the son of Godwine, who had prospered during the reign of Cnut, while his sister Eadgyth (Edith) had married Edward the Confessor (reigned 1005–66), king of England at the time of the Conquest. Earl Gyrth held one-third of Gipeswic and Queen Edith held the rest. It may be that William I wanted to make a point of some sort by attacking an important town in the kingdom, though what that point was is unclear, especially as William claimed direct legitimate succession from Edward and the compilers of the *Domesday Book* used 'the time of King Edward' as the standard test for legal rights and tenure.

An alternative theory for the sacking of Gipeswic was the final Danish raid, carried out by Sweyn of Denmark in 1069, after the Norman Conquest. In a foolish bid to re-establish Viking rule, Sweyn sailed up the Orwell and landed at Gipeswic. A ferocious fight ensued and Sweyn set fire to a large area before Sheriff Roger Bigod, who held the town for King William, drove him off.

Archaeology has so far been unable to establish the precise events of those years. Keith Wade writes that during the period of the Viking attacks 'many people died and many building sites in Ipswich have produced bits of human skeletons which could date to this time'. All over the town, skeletons have been found 'buried in haphazard fashion' though nothing is provable. Suffice it to say that, for whatever reason, Gipeswic was in a poor state when the *Domesday Book* was compiled.

For all that, the beginning of the 11th century is the first time in the history of Ipswich when there is real documentary evidence instead of supposition and archaeology. At his Christmas court of 1085, William I announced his intention to make an inventory of the new kingdom which, since it was only a few years into his reign, was in reality an inventory of the Anglo-Saxons. Commissioners were sent out to seven ordained circuits – the Eastern circuit being Suffolk, Norfolk and Essex – to assess the value (and thereby the taxable revenue) of the realm.

The commissioners were disappointed to find that Gipeswic's tax revenue was somewhat depleted as a result of the sacking of the town. Before 1055 there were 538 burgesses who had paid the 'customary due to the king', but at Domesday there were only 110 burgesses who paid and 100 who could afford nothing at all 'apart from one penny'. There were 328 dwellings 'laid waste', on which no tax at all was paid.

There was also a decline in fortunes for the town mint. The commissioners recorded that before 1066 the moneyers had paid £4 a year, and 'now they ought to pay £20, but of four years' [money] they have paid only £27'. Quite why Sheriff Bigod expected such an exorbitant amount from a derelict mint is unexplained since the moneyers were no better off than the burgesses.

Coins had been minted at Gipeswic since at least the time of Edgar, who was responsible for inaugurating a reform of the coinage and increasing the number of minting places. Whether Gipeswic was a new

A King John short-cross silver penny of the Ipswich mint, the moneyer named as Johan.on.Gipes (Johan of Ipswich) (Lockdales).

mint or a reformed mint is unknown but since it was one of the principal political and commercial centres of the kingdom of East Anglia it is possible that there was an even earlier one. There is evidence of silver-working in the seventh century so there would have been men in the town familiar with the malleable metal of the coinage. There was one national currency, which circulated throughout England, and the number of mints was always carefully controlled, with permission to strike coins granted sparingly. Coins struck at Gipeswic were not used there exclusively and 10th-century coins have been found in Norfolk, Hertfordshire, Hampshire, Kent, Sussex and Dorset.

Throughout the turbulent years of the 10th and 11th centuries the Gipeswic moneyers continued their work, though exactly where is not known for certain. Two sites are mooted as the most likely: one is along Upper Orwell Street, in the Cox Lane car park area; and the other is at the western end of the Buttermarket, where the famous Ipswich silver pennies turned up.

Coins bearing the bust of Cnut were found in the historic Beauworth (Hampshire) hoard discovered in 1833. They were among 8,000 coins from 65 mints, each coin carrying not only a bust of the ruler but also the name of the mint and the moneyer. Thus, the earliest Ipswich people for whom we have names are the Gipeswic moneyers. Mostly they are Anglo-Saxon names such as Aelwine, Godric, Leofrinc, Lifinge and Thvrstan. Later, under Henry I (reigned 1100–35), the moneyer was Osbern, who appears again on coins minted under Stephen (reigned 1135–54) together with Alain and David. Gipeswic appears on the coins in various forms – Gipis, Gipeswi, Gi and Gipes among others (but appears as Gepeswiz in the *Domesday Book*).

At the time of the Conquest the moneyer was Aethelbeorht, and Aelfric was the moneyer by the time of William II (reigned 1087–1100). One or both these of men were required by the Sheriff to pay the impossible £20. However, since at least 12 moneyers appear on William I pennies minted at Gipeswic it is to be presumed that Roger Bigod had the mint up and running very soon after taking charge. When Henry II came to the throne in 1154 Gipeswic was designated one of the royal mints and some of the names on these pennies also appear on London-minted coins, suggesting promotion to the capital for some of the moneyers.

The Ipswich mint continued until around 1254, when Henry III (reigned 1216–72) made far-reaching reforms to the coinage, but had ceased by the time Edward I (reigned 1272–1307) carried out his grand re-coinage, when many scattered workshops of the moneyers were centralised.

Following the Conquest, the Bigod family fortunes quickly flourished in Gipeswic. Roger was the son of a Norman knight, Robert le Bigod, who distinguished himself at the Battle of Hastings. The Bigods were duly rewarded with 117 manors in Suffolk as well as the Sheriffdom of Gipeswic. One of the three mediaeval quays of the ancient town was named Bigod's Quay and his descendants became earls of Norfolk in the 12th century. Roger Bigod, 5th Earl of Norfolk, was one of the most powerful barons in Edward I's reign. It was Hugh Bigod, Sheriff Bigod's son, who built the now vanished, and somewhat mysterious, Ipswich Castle.

Its structure can only be guessed at by looking at other Bigod castles (Bungay, Walton and Framlingham) and the site of its construction is a mystery. That it existed is not disputed, since it was besieged in 1153 by King Stephen (reigned 1135–54) and its destruction was ordered in 1176 by Henry II (reigned 1154–89), the first of the Plantagenet kings. An episode in the civil war that raged in Anglo-Norman England during Stephen's reign was played out in Ipswich, chiefly because of the chameleonic nature of the powerful Bigod loyalty. Stephen had granted the Earldom of Suffolk and Norfolk to Hugh Bigod, who promptly showed his gratitude by siding with Henry of Anjou in his battle with Stephen in the matter of the succession. Ipswich Castle was one of many such structures dotted across the county, built not so much for defence but to show the population who was in charge. Historians agree that it was probably built of stone with a simple motte-and-bailey design, resembling a fortified manor house rather than a turreted castle. The original may well have been wooden and parts of it rebuilt with stone over time. As a tactic of his cause, Stephen laid siege to numerous castles across East Anglia, including Bigod's Ipswich stronghold. The siege succeeded and in 1153 it became a royal castle, in the possession of King Stephen. Henry's forces took it back again, at which point Hugh Bigod changed sides and wrested it back for Stephen.

By 1154, though, Henry of Anjou had been crowned Henry II and the Bigods were obliged to surrender it to the king. However, when Henry's eldest son rebelled in 1173, Hugh Bigod illogically threw in his lot with the rebel. He allowed the mercenary Flemish army to use Ipswich as a base but eventually had to make his peace with the king and pay a hefty

St Mary Stoke is one of the 12 remaining mediaeval churches and is close to the original site of Anglo-Saxon Gipeswic.

Medallions on the Town Hall depict King Richard, Cardinal Wolsey and King John under figures representing commerce, agriculture, law and learning, and justice.

fine. In an act of revenge against Bigod's betrayal, Henry ordered that Ipswich Castle be 'razed to the ground', being justly sceptical about the Bigods' loyalty. There must also have been considerable damage to the castle's structure, which Henry might simply have considered a drain on his purse.

The question of where this castle stood is still outstanding. One of the most popular theories is that it was somewhere near the church of St Mary le Tower. There is little to support this other than 'le Tower', which likely refers to a smaller tower on the earthen ramparts since it was already named *Sc Maria ad Turrim* (St Mary at the Tower) in the *Domesday Book*.

Keith Wade suggests the most likely place was on Elm Street and that St Mary at Elms was the original chapel for the castle. There is

St Mary le Tower has been the town church since at least the 12th century.

much logic to support this but no physical evidence other than the unusual curve of Elm Street. It might be supposed that ashlar fragments would be found incorporated into nearby buildings, even in St Mary's itself. However, while there is Norman masonry to be found it is minimal and does not suggest the remains of a castle. No other building has, so far, been found to contain significant amounts of the lost castle of Hugh Bigod.

As the 13th century hove into view, the port of Ipswich had swarming quays overseen by a flourishing group of merchants, the town centre was a milieu of markets, shops and houses, and the economy was expanding. The new Norman order took firm hold of the town, encouraging the growth of religious orders. The earthen town ramparts were built and rebuilt, and before long the entrance to the town would be guarded by four gates – north, south, east and west – the northern aspect linked by the ramparts forming an arc that can still be seen today in Crown Street and Tower Ramparts. It was an exciting, vibrant place to be and no wonder that it attracted the attention of King John, who was to put, in the time-honoured cliché, the icing on the cake.

CHAPTER THREE

KING JOHN AND THE CHARTER

When King John (reigned 1199–1216) ascended the throne, the exchequer was desperately short of funds. The cost of the late King Richard's crusades and the French wars meant that the new king had to find a way of boosting funds. Granting charters to thriving towns was one way of raising money and Ipswich, with its busy port and expanding reputation for successful trade, fitted the bill. King Richard (reigned 1189–99) had granted some privileges, but in 1200 the impoverished King John bestowed a royal charter on the town.

Ipswich is unusual among the early charter towns in that it immediately resolved that the proceedings should be recorded and a full account of events was recorded in an Ipswich *Domesday Book*. Although a roguish clerk named John le Blake stole the document in 1272, its contents were already noted. A new copy was made some years later, and in 1290 a committee was elected to recollect the customs and compile another Domesday roll to be called the *Little Domesday Book of Ipswich*. In many ways John le Blake did the town a favour since it is likely that the very early records could anyway have been lost by reasons of neglect or misuse down the centuries. It brought to the burgesses' attention what could happen and care was taken of the rolls. In the 14th century it would appear that more than one copy was made, the second intended as a working copy. It was obviously important to the town leaders from the beginning that records were made and preserved.

The charter was sealed on 25 May 1200 and on 29 June the King's Charter was read to a crowd of assembled personages in the churchyard of St Mary le Tower on what was the most auspicious day in the history of Ipswich. An account was entered in the Domesday ledger: 'On

Townspeople gathered in St Mary le Tower churchyard to hear King John's Charter in 1200.

Thursday, next after the Feast of the Nativity of St John the Baptist, the whole town of the Borough of Ipswich assembled in the burial-ground of St Mary at the Tower, to elect two Bailiffs and four Coroners in the same borough, according to the form of the Charters of the same Lord the King, which the same King hath lately granted to the Burgesses of the borough aforesaid.'

The town was empowered to elect 'two of the more lawful and discreet men of their town' who would represent them and 'who may well and faithfully keep the government at the Borough of Ipswich'. This they did and after swearing faithfully 'to keep the said Charter and to deliver it to the said town when it shall be necessary' the men were entrusted with the charter document. Those elected to become the new town hierarchy were John Fitz-Norman, William de Belines, Philip da Porta and Roger Lew. They would keep their offices only so long as they were 'of good behaviour'.

The burgesses were further granted the right to choose their own officers and to pay the borough's annual rent – or *farm*, as it was called – directly to the royal exchequer.

The following week the bailiffs, coroners and Portmen (12 men elected to maintain the borough liberties) met to draw up plans for government. A town seal was commissioned for use on important civic business and for sealing letters. The King's Charter was once more read in public, this time to the county courts of both Suffolk and Norfolk, so that all and sundry should know the new judicial order. Where previously all the profits of justice, such as fines and forfeitures awarded by the courts, went to the crown they were henceforth entitled to be used for the benefit of the town.

Once the charter was enacted, the town ceased to be governed under the king's stewardship and would, henceforth, have a new system of elected representatives who would have certain responsibilities as well as rights. The 12 Portmen were given the right to graze their horses on the meadows known as Oldenholm, which later became known as the Portman Marshes and is today marked as Portman Road, the home ground of Ipswich Town Football Club.

Another important right was permission for a merchant guild, and on 12 October another meeting was held to elect an alderman of the guild. A guild consisted of men and women from religious or craft fraternities offering mutual help and succour to its members. In 1325 the guild was reconstituted as the Corpus Christi Guild, which became the most prestigious among the town's religious fellowship. The town clergy played a leading role from its base at St Mary le Tower, holding various feasts throughout the year at St Mildred's Chapel. Members of the Guild performed in the Mystery (or Miracle) Plays – cycles of plays dramatising key biblical stories from the Creation and the Fall of Man to the Last Judgement. After the pope forbade clergy to act in public in 1210, performances were taken over by the guilds and Ipswich was one of the towns where the plays were regularly performed.

In the ensuing years the Charter was amended, rescinded and adapted by succeeding monarchs as it pleased them so to do. It was a fine way of raising extra taxes – first remove the Charter and then return it for an appropriate fee. Edward I (reigned 1272–1307), for example, declared himself displeased with the performances of the bailiffs and took the town back, not restoring it until 1291 when Ipswich had provided men for the king's ships. More problems occurred in 1344 when Edward III (reigned 1327–1377) was apprised of a potential scandal over what was seen as too lenient justice afforded a group of smugglers, and the king once more used the royal prerogative. By and large, though, the basic rights and privileges of the administration derived from the Charter and were acceptable to the townspeople. The traders also welcomed it, as did the merchants, whose export and import businesses were enhanced by the town's status. As early as 1280 the port had sufficient traffic to warrant the appointment of a collector of customs.

Unsurprisingly, the names Bigod and Malet, two Norman families who had held Ipswich for William I, appear on the list of barons who attended the historic meeting at the High Altar of the Benedictine Abbey in Bury St Edmunds on 20 November 1214. Under the pretext of pilgrimage to the shrine of St Edmund, 25 barons of England took an oath that they would compel King John to grant them their lawful rights, by force of arms if need be. Some months later, at Runnymede on 15 June 1215, the king signed the document known the world over as the Magna Carta (Great Charter).

It was by no means the end of the story, as the king predictably reneged on his promises and gathered his forces to bring the barons into line. He persuaded the pope to declare the Magna Carta invalid but within a few months he was dead and succeeded by his nine-year-old son, Henry. King John is believed to have made only one visit to Ipswich, in 1216, a year after the signing of the Magna Carta.

The expanding mercantile port that Ipswich had become inevitably began to attract the religious communities that were arriving in Britain from continental Europe. The first to arrive were the Augustinians, known as the Black Canons, whose house was founded by Henry I in 1130 in St Peter's parish. There had been a church there since before the Norman Conquest, and the sight of the friars in their black cassocks and hooded black cloaks among the merchants and seamen milling around the docks became an increasingly familiar sight.

The advent of the mendicant friars (from the Latin *mendicare* meaning to beg) in the 12th and 13th centuries contributed to the character of Ipswich. They were, after all, part of town life for some 400 years and originally depended entirely on voluntary contributions or alms. The mendicant orders did not build imposing abbeys, as the Benedictines did at Bury St Edmunds and Norwich, so the town has no grand ruins or a magnificent cathedral. Instead, the friars relied on the charity of the townspeople and rich merchants for their keep. No wonder that they were attracted to Ipswich. It would be pointless to beg on the streets of a rundown or impoverished town. It was far better to go where there were wealthy patrons to house them and alms to sustain their charitable enterprises.

In return for temporalities, the friars offered prayers for the donors' souls (both in life and death), ministered to the poor and destitute, and offered hospitality to travellers. The Black Canons soon found their duty of care to visitors onerous in the extreme since those arriving by sea found their house all too easily. As patron the king expected all members of his court to be cared for, an opportunity taken advantage of by both kings and courtiers, which put an intolerable strain on the resources of the canons. Gradually, however, the priory received gifts of land in the town, and in 1303 money was granted to expand the priory. A second house was opened well away from the quayside – Holy Trinity Priory, outside the town ramparts close to the North Gate on the site of the present day Christchurch Mansion – and Edward III later granted dispensation from the hospitality rule.

The next to arrive were the Dominicans, also known as the Blackfriars, or Friars Preacher. They wore a black cloak over a white habit and established themselves just north of St Mary at Quay in 1263.

The ruins of Blackfriars Friary are the only permanent reminder of the pre-Reformation religious houses.

The Dominicans were an international brotherhood of individuals who had arrived in England in 1221 having been dispersed throughout Western Europe to study theology and preach against heresy.

By now the population of Ipswich was becoming denser. Suburbs were beginning to spring up outside the ramparts, such as the parishes of St Helen and St Matthew, and traffic increased around the four main entrance gates. The town itself did not grow significantly but the population did. The street grid system laid down in Anglo-Saxon times remained, and the houses, priories and public buildings were fitted into the available space. The increase in building provided work for the craftsmen. In 1335 a brick extension was built onto St Mildred's Chapel and included an external flight of stone steps. The chapel was no longer consecrated and had become a seat of local government. In the same year the burgesses petitioned the king for confirmation of their charters and to ask permission to 'approve and build on the waste and waste places in the town'.

The question of land rights was ongoing. Who was lord of the waste soil of a borough – the body of burgesses or the king? Often the questions went unanswered and the borough acted 'on their own warrant', with the land parcelled and leased or sold. The borough had a duty to self-finance and the waste, or unused, land within the town was an increasingly important asset as the demand for building increased and the amount of available land decreased.

There was also the problem of increasing numbers of ships bringing ever more goods to the port, necessitating constant improvements to the revetments for loading and unloading cargo. The river's edge once ran along what is now College Street, but over the years there were changing tide levels and a series of high tides meant severe flooding in the warehouses and private dwellings along the quays. This continual shoring up of the revetments meant that the quayside gradually encroached further into the river. The revetments are found to have been a series of wooden posts and wattle hurdles filled in behind with earth or rubble and added to as the need arose. They were made higher and stronger, relentlessly building up the waterfront during the whole of the mediaeval period.

Thanks to a newly discovered map of 'Gippeswiche', dated 1539 and therefore earlier than Speed's map of 1610, it seems that there was some kind of gatehouse on both the north and south sides of Stoke bridge, probably to monitor traffic and impose an entry tax or port charge. The Stoke crossing had been a physical barrier to shipping coming up the Orwell since its construction late in the seventh century (or before). Once in place it was a key point of entry and exit in the important trade route to all markets south, especially London and Kent. In security terms control points at the bridge entrance acted as a fifth town gate and a similar building can be discerned as still there on Ogilby's 1674 survey. Henry VIII commissioned the 1539 map at a time when he feared invasion by France and Spain. He was aware of the vulnerability of the Suffolk coast and detailed notes are made of the entrance to the Orwell.

It is not known if the third group of friars came by ship or overland, but they were the Whitefriars, or Carmelites, who gained their name from the white cloak worn over a brown habit. Arriving in 1278 they found the St Peter's site taken by the Augustinians, and the Dominicans beginning to expand their house in the Foundation Street area, so chose a less crowded area just south of the Buttermarket, which eventually extended from Queen Street to St Stephen's Lane.

Lastly came the Franciscans (or Greyfriars), who arrived in the 1290s and settled in the parish of St Nicholas. They were to become the most popular of the friars and as a result gained both money and gifts in kind. There was a constant tussle of conscience among the friars who were bound to follow the example of St Francis in the rule of poverty to the exclusion of all else, including learning. Poverty was an end in itself, decreed St Francis, and must not entail education, which needed money to sustain it. Books were required, as were houses for the books, and proper food was needed to sustain study. On the other hand it was impractical for the friars to live on the streets and go barefoot all year round and many saw theological study as acceptable. Also, walking the streets without footwear would have been equally unpleasant in winter, when the mud would have made a 'pudding' with the street waste, as in summer, when the dust would lay over the rotting waste, making it prudent to pick a way carefully through the mess. Going about after dark was even more treacherous.

Gradually, the avowed rule of apostolic poverty was perforce watered down and most of the Franciscans found a compromise by living in, but not owning, their friaries and allowing poverty and learning to co-exist. They served the poor and wretched wherever and whenever they could and were sought-after as confessors. Such was their popularity that it began to annoy local priests, who watched jealously as the townspeople flocked to hear the Franciscans preach and reward them with alms, property and esteem.

The Dominicans were not so popular. Having a declared interest in serious and profound theological study, their material needs were greater, and they had to attract richer patrons. Also, their somewhat pompous and 'holier than thou' preaching was not as appealing as that of the gentler, more listener-friendly Franciscans.

By the end of the 13th century, Ipswich was awash with friars and they became as much a part of town life as the merchants, the dockworkers, the market stallholders, the town clerks and borough officials, together with the innkeepers and itinerant travellers.

The church, too, was flourishing as it continued to increase its influence in the life of the nation. A good measure of mediaeval church-building in Ipswich is the dominance of church towers on the town skyline, even today. From Turret Street it is just possible to see St Mary le Tower, St Stephen's and St Lawrence's, with St Mary at Quay and St

Peter's just out of sight. Twelve mediaeval churches survive in the town, a visible testament to the density of population. All would have mustered sizeable congregations and, therefore, tidy sums in the collection boxes.

The religion of the day was Roman Catholicism and the mass was said in Latin. People would congregate in the church nave during services – which would follow a familiar pattern – giving the responses in a 'dead' language not their own. The ringing of a bell and wafting of incense signified the solemn moments of the mass. The walls and windows of the church bore images of the saints and scenes from the life of Christ, which served as their guide and inspiration. It was a universal church that facilitated the in-coming friars, who were able to celebrate mass whatever their nationality. Mediaeval Christianity formed the boundaries and codes for everyday life in England and across Europe so it blended imperceptibly into all political structures.

Throughout the ups and down of national politics, the people of Ipswich got on with the necessary job of wealth creation. In the 13th century wool was an important commodity and formed a link between the town and the surrounding farm. Mark Bailey writes that 'wool was sold for commercial profit on almost every Suffolk manor where sheep were reared'. Fleeces were sold to merchants, who sold them on in a single batch. In the 1280s wool was one of the chief taxable goods of the Ipswich residents and it became the centre of higher-quality cloth, woven for a wealthy clientele. Later, a secondary mass market opened up when cloth of a lesser standard was produced for the 'lower orders' of society.

By the 15th century the town merchants were trading as far away as Spain and Italy. Huge quantities of fish were being caught both offshore and in Icelandic waters, where a third of the boats originated from Suffolk. An intriguing snapshot of late 14th-century Ipswich is found in *The Canterbury Tales* by Geoffrey Chaucer (c.1340–1400). Chaucer's family ran a tavern (in Tavern Street) during the 13th and 14th centuries and, although there is no proof that he ever visited Ipswich, he wrote of the 'forked beard' merchants who sailed the seas 'betwixe Middelburgh and Orewelles'. They wore the 'Flandrish beaver hat' that was seen to be sported by most fashionable merchants of the day.

In December 1296 the town witnessed a most prestigious visit by Edward I, nicknamed 'Edward Longshanks' due to his unusual height. One of his 14 children, Princess Elizabeth, was married to the Count of Holland in the town and thousands of London visitors, wedding guests, troops, craftsmen and women, jewellers, minstrels and members of the royal entourage flooded in for the occasion. Meticulous accounts were compiled as a means of ascertaining the cost of the marriage, some of which survive in the British Museum. Edward could ill-afford such an ostentatious display but lack of funds did not prevent him, or any other mediaeval monarch before or after, from putting on a show of wealth and majesty. John Wodderspoon wrote that 'the entire population, residents and strangers, followed one course of unbroken feasting and enjoyment'.

The king's almoner dispensed gifts to the town's poor and to the various friaries to enable them to celebrate the wedding. The only incident to mar the proceedings was a violent display of temper by the king, who threw his daughter's coronet into the fire. Two precious stones were lost and the king's goldsmith was summoned to replace them with 'a large ruby and a large emerald'.

The town and port of Ipswich continued to experience the ups and downs of the mediaeval economy, which included wine, hides, wool, cloth and fish, and during the 1470s trade fell away badly. The quays fell into such disrepair that the burgesses had to apportion funds for patching them up. Disease, most notably the plague, often visited the town, brought in easily by the sea-going traffic and leaving people in perpetual fear of its return.

Edward I displayed an ongoing interest in Gipeswic and in 1925 commissioned the building of a galley, the earliest vessel built in Ipswich. It was logical that such a burgeoning port would soon spawn a shipyard and subsidiary industries, such as rope-making. Rope was essential for shipping, farming and industry and there were many rope works over the years. Only one remains, in name only. The area around Rope Walk was the oldest and largest of the town's ropewalks.

Mark Bailey points to the town's other main function at the time, which was 'to serve as the centre of the county's administration and system of justice'. This was an increasingly important function and the sophisticated nature of the borough came to breed men of ambition, but one man above all was ambition personified. Thomas Wolsey was a man of his time, epitomising those who were able to rise from humble beginnings to walk the corridors of power.

CHAPTER FOUR

RISE AND FALL OF THOMAS WOLSEY

Thomas Wolsey (*c.* 1472–1530) was not only the most prominent person to emerge from mediaeval Gipeswic but also, after Henry VIII, the most powerful man in the kingdom and probably the most famous of all Ipswichians. He dominated both the political and ecclesiastical life of the nation from around 1515 to a year before his death. He entered the royal service when the young and vigorous Henry VIII ascended the throne in 1509, aged only 18. Wolsey cleverly sought to remove from his sovereign that part of kingship that he so disliked, the business of government. Wolsey was at the king's side when he rode into the spectacular Field of Cloth of Gold in 1520, a pageant masterminded by Wolsey from the construction of the tents down to the food and drink required for 5,000 guests, and for which Henry was well pleased. England was emptied of its jewels and precious materials in an attempt to woo the French king. As a diplomatic offensive it failed, but Wolsey had proved himself worthy of the royal trust, allowing Henry to abdicate the bureaucracy of kingship and hand it over to him, a situation that prevailed until the king wanted to divest himself of his queen.

Wolsey's birth date and place are both uncertain, but his family moved from St Mary Elms to the parish of St Nicholas and lived in a house not dissimilar to Curson Lodge. His father was a tavern keeper and butcher in the town and much has been written about his business methods and ability to sail close to the wind when it came to upholding the rules of the meat markets. The family attended the Church of St Nicholas and the young Thomas grew up well versed in the ways of both religion and commerce. He would have heard his father talk of trade and business matters and learned how a prosperous borough was administered.

The family lived close to the Shrine Chapel of Our Lady of Grace (where Lady Lane now is), with young Thomas no doubt impressed by the numerous and often grand visitors. The chapel contained a statue of the Blessed Virgin Mary and had welcomed pilgrims since at least the early 13th century. Men and women from all walks of life were constantly abroad in the town, bringing with them a taste of the wider world. They stayed in the inns and told tales of other pilgrimage sites across Europe, at a time when all of Christendom was united by a single religion. Perhaps it was a vicarious ambition to be part of that exciting world that decided Robert Wolsey to educate his son and provide every possible opportunity for his advancement. He did well: Thomas was a brilliant student and in due course began his meteoric rise from a senior cleric to cardinal, then to the Lord Chancellor of England and finally Archbishop of Canterbury.

The contrast between his lowly beginnings and his new life turned his head. Through an increasing air of superiority and self-congratulation he earned almost universal loathing from even his closest associates. His

An early 20th-century view of St Peter's Church and an ivy-clad Wolsey's Gate.

household numbered in excess of 500 and, wrote his biographer, Cavendish, 'in his time of authority and glory, he was the haughtiest of men in all his proceedings that then lived, having more respect to the worldly honour of his person than he had to his spiritual profession'.

Those who despised him, or were jealous, rarely missed an opportunity to remind him of his origins, referring to 'the butcher's boy' or 'the butcher's dog'. He travelled with a considerable entourage, preceded by massive silver crosses with his cardinal's hat carried before him.

It was recorded that Wolsey became 'courted, bribed, and caressed by the greatest potentates in Christendom. In virtue of his authority as pope's legate, he instituted an inquisitorial court, in which he exercised a power not known before in England. He so absolutely governed the king.'

When a local boy makes such a phenomenal success of his career he invariably returns to his native town in triumph, especially if possessed of such conceit as Wolsey. From about 1526, when a Papal Bull was granted for the establishment of a new college, arrangements were put in hand for the founding of Wolsey's 'Saint Mary, Cardynall College of Ipswich'. It was to consist of a school (with a master and eight ushers), a president, 12 fellows, clerks and a number of priests. At first, Wolsey wanted the college to be close to the Shrine Chapel of Our Lady, near to the West Gate, which had grown in status since the visit of Catharine of Aragon (in 1517) and the pilgrimage by Henry VIII in 1522 (both of whom stayed at Curson House, on the corner of Silent Street and St Peter's Street). In an effort to save money, however, a site close to St Peter's Church was chosen and soon afterwards the church was seized and re-designated the College Chapel. A considerable complex was planned to accommodate the school and the attendant masters and clergy, and it was to be linked with Wolsey's Oxford College.

Pope Clement VII authorised the dissolution of seven lesser priories in Suffolk and Norfolk and their assets were used to help pay for Wolsey's

The weathered royal arms of Henry VIII above the recently renovated gatehouse.

grandiose scheme. The Augustinian priory of St Peter and Paul was suppressed and parishioners of St Peter's were told to go elsewhere, either to St Nicholas or St Mary Quay. Parts of the old priory were to be re-used and would, therefore, extend north and east of where St Peter's Church still stands.

Huge quantities of stone were ordered from the Caen quarries, as well as timber and lead for the roofs, and on 15 June 1528 the foundation stone was laid. The influential Daundy family were cousins of Wolsey and local grandees, conscious of the privilege soon to be bestowed and so were keen to lend support. In August the town Portmen wrote to Wolsey in gratitude for the honour he had bestowed on his place of birth. Gifts of vestments and books were sent from donors across the county and beyond, and Wolsey himself sent furnishings from his London house, York Place. Money was set apart for everything from wine, wax, bedding, choristers' apparel, horses, kitchen equipment and household staff to repairs to the existing structures and provision for the secular canons and clerks.

Determined to benefit from the celebrated Shrine of Our Lady, Wolsey decreed that a grand pageant to the chapel should mark the college opening. After all, Henry VII had made several visits even before those of Queen Catherine and Henry VIII. The procession was to take place on the 8 September in celebration of the Nativity of the Blessed Virgin Mary and was intended to rival that of the town's Corpus Christi guild and, indeed, any other such procession in the town's history. Wolsey sent Dr Stephen Gardiner and Dr Rowland Lee to Ipswich with 'rich copes, fine vestments and magnificent jewels and ornaments' and instructions to make the occasion one to remember.

By September 1528 a number of boys were already under tuition and were to join the pageant, along with college staff, priests, clerks, choristers, town officials, the Prior of Christchurch and 'gentlemen of the county'. As a practice run for the opening ceremony, the company made a procession along the prescribed route to the chapel for Evensong 'upon Our Ladye's Eve' – that is, 7 September. William Capon (the first and last dean of the college) reported to Wolsey that it had all gone very well and that college hospitality had been offered to the dignitaries present 'where they were entertained with the best wine'.

Ominously, Monday 8 September was a day of unremitting, relentless rain. It is still not known if anyone processed to the chapel, but it is doubtful that Dean Capon would have risked exposing either the Cardinal's precious vestments or the assembled company to the dreadful weather. The dean wrote to Wolsey that the weather had been 'fowle wedder' and it had 'rayned sore contynewally', and while admitting that the entire pageant had not taken place he tried to smooth things over by reporting that they 'made as solemn a procession in your Grace's college as could be devysed'. Many 'respectable personages' attended and, in an effort to pacify the cardinal, the dean named as many of these personages as possible.

Wolsey must have been very disappointed that his grand plan had gone so awry and that the people of Ipswich had missed the opportunity to be impressed by the opulence of what was, in effect, the glorification not so much of the new college but of Wolsey himself. But, as it turned out, it hardly mattered. Less than a year later Henry had dismissed Wolsey from his Chancellorship after the cardinal's failure to procure the king's divorce from Queen Catherine.

Wolsey's fall from grace was swift and with him went the Ipswich College. Although the new building was suitably advanced and the town beginning to bask in its newly illuminated role in the life of the nation, it was not sufficiently established to withstand the demise of its chief patron. Indeed, it is probable that Wolsey himself never saw the college and was intending to make a grand entrance at a later date, perhaps accompanied by the king. Instead, he was indicted of *praemunire*, a charge of exercising unlawful jurisdiction in England, and arrested. Having sought shelter in Leicester Abbey, he died there on 29 November 1530 (some say by his own hand), thus depriving his enemies the chance to witness his death by the executioner's axe.

Several months before Wolsey's death, however, the king's men were in Ipswich taking an inventory of the college assets and, in spite of entreaties by Gardiner, he ordered the suppression of the Cardinal's College. The half-built site was passed to Thomas Alvard, Henry VIII's paymaster in Westminster, and the buildings dismantled and taken by sea to London for use in the building that was to become Whitehall. Stone from Caen, Kent and Rygate was removed, along with timbers (turned, carved and some gilded) and glasswork. It is said that the king was enraged that Wolsey had put his own coat of arms above his on the main college door and resolved to raze it to the ground.

Desperate to save something from the situation, the borough recovered the school's endowment, which had been left to the town's grammar school in the 15th century by Richard Felaw. The king was persuaded to refound the school in the town (now Ipswich School), and the master at the Cardinal's College, William Golding, stayed on under the new regime.

All that is left of the Cardinal's College is a short length of wall and the Tudor brick doorway bearing the arms of Henry VIII that fronts on to College Street. They are suggestions of what might have been if Wolsey had started his project sooner, as both the structure and a working college would have been less easy to dismantle. The parishioners of St Peter's petitioned for the return of their church and regained it in 1536.

There was to be a profound aftermath to Wolsey's suppression of the minor priories: the king saw how he could replenish his exchequer by suppressing the great abbeys and priories belonging to the religious orders. Denied his divorce from Catherine, Henry split with the Church of Rome and founded a new Church of England with himself as the Supreme Head. He effectively granted his own divorce and secretly married Anne Boleyn. In 1538 a cataclysmic upheaval in the kingdom was triggered, as royal commissioners were sent out to ransack the religious houses, confiscating everything they owned, their inmates pensioned off or made to join the parish clergy. Many ended their days on the streets. The monasteries held a quarter of the land in the country and it was not difficult for the king to manipulate the increasing anti-clerical mood in parliament.

Change was afoot. The wandering preacher Thomas Bilney caused a great stir in the town during 1527 when he promoted the Protestant doctrines of Wycliffe and Luther, which had made the friars so angry that they dragged him out of the pulpit of St George's Chapel. The population was becoming more literate and Ipswich, a primary point of contact with the rest of Europe, was one of the ports through which forbidden and unbound Protestant literature had been smuggled. A Frisian, Reginald Oliver, is credited as being the first to set up a publishing house in the town (in 1534), with Anthony Scoloker setting up the first Ipswich printing press in 1547.

In Ipswich the commissioners visited the Holy Trinity priory during 1536 and took an inventory of the few possessions they had. The house was closed the next year, followed by those of the Carmelites and Dominicans and then the Franciscans. The zealous supporters of the New Religion turned the people against the friars and made it impossible for them to beg for alms. By the end of 1538 all the friaries were either dismantled or in the hands of new, secular owners.

Although the friars had become unpopular during Henry's reign, the people were nevertheless unprepared for the sweeping changes that took place during the 1540s. For around 300 years the friars had been woven into the fabric of Ipswich and there were many who had benefitted from their activities. The church was a very visual affair, literacy being the prerogative of the few, and they were shocked to see the icons smashed by the reformers, the images of the saints defaced, and sacred tokens stolen or removed to the king's treasury. Their religion came through the elaborate wall paintings and stained glass depicting scripture and the life of Christ. The shrines, such as the Shrine Chapel in Lady Lane, were draped with gifts or with rags from those who had been cured by miracles wrought in the name of the saints. The images of Our Lady were gilded and revered as holy. These things were stripped from the church fabric and there was no redress. The king's authority was absolute and few dared to question the royal commissioners as they loaded up their carts with gold and silver, which parishioners and patrons had given freely over the years to glorify God's houses on earth. The libraries were similarly vandalised, with books either sold or destroyed. The golden statue of Our Lady was stripped of its magnificent cape, jewels and silver shoes, and taken to London, where it was burnt along with those of Our Lady of Walsingham, Worcester and Wilsden. To make matters worse the plague visited Gipeswic again in the 1540s.

Ipswich had survived invasion by the Romans, Vikings, Angles, Saxons and, most dramatically and profoundly, the Normans, but the events and effects of the Reformation were wrought on a well-established borough whose rule book was rewritten by the king's command. If they were to survive they had no choice but to comply with the new religious order. Among those to benefit from the Reformation were the regular clergy, some of whom were ardent supporters of the doctrines of Protestantism. The town churches had suffered competition from the religious houses, but now their fabric was gradually restored and they took on a new role within the lately hatched Church of England.

Gipeswic was now called Gippeswiche, and merchants continued to ply their prosperous trade in spite of all the changes, with exports of cloth almost doubling in volume in the early 1540s. In 1524 Ipswich ranked as the sixth or seventh-richest English town. Business was booming and the few brasses and tombs left in the town churches, and the almshouses and charities that were founded, are witness to the wealth.

The parishes of St Mary Quay and St Clement's were favourite places for the merchants to build their communities. They needed to be close to the quays, and most of the houses doubled as warehouses. Men like the great Henry Tooley (died 1550), a town benefactor whose ship the *Mary Walsingham* made frequent fishing trips to Iceland, managed to straddle the changing politics. At the start of the 16th century he was importing bales of woad and large quantities of wine, which he brought into Southampton and shipped round the coast to Ipswich. When Tooley died his will took two years to prove, but it ended with the establishment of charitable trusts that became known as the Tooley Foundation. A plaque to Henry Tooley can be seen on the wall in front of the 19th-century almshouses on Foundation Street, roughly on the site of the old 16th-century buildings.

Almshouses built in 1846 on or near the site of the original houses founded 1550.

Other wealthy men, such as the merchant and ship owner William Sabyn, took over some of the building of the old Blackfriars premises and a London merchant, Edmund Withypoll, purchased the old Trinity Priory in 1545, building what is known today as Christchurch Mansion. Thomas Seckford, a Member of Parliament for the borough, also built a 'Great House' just south of the old West Gate, where he entertained Elizabeth I.

Dark and dangerous days were to follow the Reformation. First the short-lived Edward VI (reigned 1547–53) upheld his father Henry VIII's legacy of religious reform, then Queen Mary (reigned 1553–58) attempted to restore Catholicism, passing through Ipswich on her way to claim the crown on 31 July 1553. Wodderspoon writes that Mary 'was at Ipswich upon her triumphant journey to London from Framlingham...the county of Suffolk deeply espoused the cause of Mary from revenge for the cruelties of the Protector Northumberland during Kett's rebellion, and several Protestant and many Catholic gentry supported her with their forces'.

Many who cheered her on her way would eventually come to regret it. The Marian Martyrs' Memorial in Christchurch Park recalls those Protestants who were burnt at the stake on Cornhill for their faith in the 1550s, during the fearful reign of 'Bloody' Mary.

A 1930s view of the Tudor room at Christchurch Mansion.

However, in 1558 Elizabeth succeeded to the throne and established Protestantism irrevocably. In 1560 the new queen granted a confirmatory charter to the borough and made her first visit the following year.

Ipswich had passed through the turbulent Tudor years to emerge stronger and more mature in the Elizabethan age. The improved science of mathematics was a boon to navigation, and great adventures were had as mariners explored the world in the new spirit for adventure and exploration. Somewhere along Fore Street, believed to be close to where the old Neptune Inn stands, lived the mariner Thomas Eldred. Both Thomas and his father ventured through the Straits of Magellan with the famous navigator Thomas Cavendish (died 1591), who was born in Trimley St Martin. Eldred was one of those who survived the considerable rigours of sea travel endured on the two-year expedition. They sailed westwards from Plymouth in July 1586 and travelled the world as few men had ever done before, opening up trade routes with the East Indies. Cavendish equalled Sir Francis Drake's achievement by becoming the second Englishman to sail round the world. Panels from Eldred's House can still be seen in Christchurch Mansion, one of which contains his portrait.

CHAPTER FIVE

ELIZABETHAN GIPPESWICHE
AND STUART IPSWICH

Queen Elizabeth (reigned 1558–1603) made her first visit to Ipswich in 1561, only three years into her reign, when she was still uncertain in her role as both queen and head of the English church. Her religious confusion was similar to that of her people, and although she still had a liking for much of the Catholic faith she shared her father's dislike of papal rule. Her advisers, however, determined that she should display absolute approval for Protestantism, and in her name more vandalism was wrought on church fabric. When she came to Ipswich, though, Elizabeth discovered that the town had gone too far for her liking by disposing of the old religion with undue haste. She was appalled at the laxity of the clergy, many of whom had wives who 'frequent or haunt' their lodgings, with several refusing to wear the surplice. Ministers, she said, displayed 'undiscreet behaviour' and the Bishop of Norwich (under whose jurisdiction the town then was) 'winketh at Schismaticks and Anabaptists'.

The queen was entertained by the Withypolls at Christchurch Mansion. She arrived on 6 August and remained there for six days, in the grandest manner possible. The royal habit of visiting parts of the kingdom in the summer months was an established way of getting out of London and cutting down on living expenses, since the entire court assumed guest status when on tour. Elizabeth stayed in the great houses of her wealthiest subjects, but rarely were they big enough, so many of the lower orders slept outside in tents. Unfortunately, during Elizabeth's stay at Christchurch events unfolded that diverted her from the laxity of the clergy and put her in fear for her throne.

Among the ladies of her court was Lady Catherine Grey, younger sister of the ill-fated, nine-day queen, Lady Jane Grey, who had been the designated heir of Edward VI but deposed in favour of Mary in 1553. Catherine had been a Lady of the Bedchamber at the court of Queen Mary and Elizabeth decided to keep her at court where she could maintain an eye on her. Catherine would probably have already known Ipswich since she and her sister, Jane, were the grandchildren of Mary Tudor, Henry VIII's favourite sister, after whom the *Mary Rose* warship was named. Mary had married Charles Brandon, 1st Duke of Suffolk (1485–1545), and the couple had homes in both Ipswich (a mansion in Upper Brook Street) and Westhorpe. Although Mary had married without permission from her sovereign brother the couple were eventually pardoned, after very large sums of money and jewellery changed hands and as a result of the direct intercession of Thomas Wolsey.

It was while the court was at Ipswich on the 1561 summer progress that Catherine's secret marriage to Edward Seymour, 1st Earl of Hertford, was discovered. Like her grandmother, she had not sought permission to marry, but by the time they reached Ipswich Catherine

Christchurch Mansion, built on the site of an Augustinian Priory.

was eight months pregnant and unable to hide her condition. She sought the help of Robert Dudley, brother-in-law of her dead sister, Jane. Dudley was also a member of the peripatetic court and Catherine visited him in his bedroom late at night. Fearful that he would be compromised should Elizabeth discover her visit, Dudley instantly betrayed Catherine. Outraged that the couple had not sought her permission to marry, the queen removed Lady Grey forthwith to the Tower, where she gave birth to a son. Although she was reunited with her husband under prison conditions, she died in 1568, aged only 28.

There was no proof that Catherine Grey was involved in any plot to remove Elizabeth from the throne, but the queen could not afford to take any chances. The incident, together with her displeasure at the town clergy and some disparaging remarks about the state of the town streets, combined to make her visit to Ipswich somewhat fraught.

However, the corporation took her comments about the dreadful state of the streets to heart and in 1571 an Act for paving the town was passed. At the same time the maligned Bishop of Norwich, John Parkhurst, attempted to re-organise the local parishes. Although he encouraged non-conformist practices and was labelled 'indolent, lax and unspiritual', Parkhurst nevertheless enabled the parishes to raise money to repair their churches, most of which were in a poor state. The constant upheaval during the Reformation years had left their mark on the fabric of the mediaeval buildings. Even the town church of St Mary le Tower was said to be in a deplorable condition. When Edward VI sent his commissioners to survey the Ipswich churches, they found that much of the plate and valuables that survived the Reformation had been pawned to pay for repairs.

In 1575 Elizabeth visited the county again and in 1579 spent four days in Ipswich. There is little in the town records about the later visits other than the queen's anxiety about the possibility of smallpox being rife in the town. Private collectors in the 18th and 19th centuries unfortunately looted the borough's muniment rooms leaving several gaps in the 16th-century correspondence archive. What is certain is that wherever the queen went, bells were rung and, in Ipswich, her birthday was celebrated with speeches and jollifications.

At the great assembly of troops at Tilbury Fort, in readiness to repel a Spanish invasion, Elizabeth delivered her famous speech about having the body of a feeble woman but the heart of a man. The man entrusted with her safety that day was Sir Henry Carey, the first Baron Hunsdon, holder of the office of High Steward of Ipswich, having been appointed in 1590 at the death of the previous holder, Sir Francis Walsingham. His army of protection for the royal person included 2,000 Suffolk men, many from Ipswich. Ipswich shipyards also supplied two ships for the Armada fleet, paying the cost by mortgaging the Portmen's meadows.

In the 1550s it became common for preachers to deliver very long, self-improving sermons, as part of the move away from the incense-swinging days of the Latin mass and towards the Puritan ideal. Elizabeth might have thought religious reform too severe, but the Puritans were of the opinion that things had not gone far enough. These were people who wanted to purify, or further reform, the church. Since they were particularly influential among the merchant classes it is not surprising that in Ipswich the ethos was embraced wholeheartedly. Ipswich's Puritan stance continued up to and throughout the English Civil War and attracted famous non-conformists such as George Fox (1624–1691), founder of the Society of Friends, to the town.

The town endorsed Queen Elizabeth's order that in addition to the Sunday sermons, extras sermons were to be delivered on Wednesdays and Fridays. All the townspeople had to attend and members of the corporation were required to wear their official robes. Taxes were imposed to pay the lecturers' salaries, and any burgess who refused to pay lost his right as a freeman of the borough. Lectures – or, more properly, sermons – were designed to give a lead on social and educational questions and were of interminable length. Some lasted several hours, during which business activity in the town ceased. Such was the interference of the Town Council in these sermons that they came into direct conflict with the Bishop of Norwich, and in 1637 there were riots against the bishop's officers.

The most famous of the Town Lecturers, the Revd Samuel Ward (1577–1640), is described by Lilian Redstone as 'silver tongued'. Ward, with his 'downright speaking and his homey metaphor' captured audiences like no other, from his appointment in 1605 until his death in 1640.

As the Elizabethan era drew to a close, Ipswich was holding its own as one of the most important provincial ports in the land. Shipbuilding was increasing and Robert Malster records that the town was known as 'the shipyard of London'. Woollen cloth was still exported, with the cloth industry expanding during the latter part of the 16th century.

The physical aspect of the town was also changing. In 1603 a new gate was added close to the West Gate and throughout the 16th century

The Ancient House on the Buttermarket.

The Courtyard is still visible from inside the Ancient House.

the ramparts were constantly repaired. It must, though, have been something of a blessing to the borough that earthen walls and ditches were easier and cheaper to maintain than stone or brick structures.

The merchants' houses were adapted and modernised as their owners grew richer. The building known today as the Ancient House was bought in 1567 by George and Mary Copping, who enlarged the modest mediaeval dwelling into a grand family home. Its elaborate pargeted ornamentation was put there later by the ardent Royalist Sparrowe family, showing the four known continents (Australia was then undiscovered) and the arms of Charles II. It is ironic that one of the most photographed and famous buildings in Ipswich should bear the royal arms of the House of Stuart when the town was so vehemently Puritan during the Civil War.

Unable to bestow their wealth on the churches or the friaries, as they might have done in pre-Reformation days, the Elizabethan merchants instead lavished their money on good living and impressive houses. The way to the top of society was no longer via the church, as in Wolsey's time, but by access to the court and the nobility.

In addition to the new religious and social identities came another cultural dimension – the emergence of popular theatre. Whereas the church had previously been the patron of arts and learning, especially

Mannings is one of the oldest buildings on Cornhill.

through the mediaeval Mystery Plays, culture now took a secular turn and Ipswich established what was to be an enduring and strong liking for the theatre. The town's nobility brought players from France, Italy and Turkey to entertain their guests. Ipswich was popular with the travelling players on two counts. First, the port saw a good number of players who passed through on their way to the Low Countries, and second they were well received. They invariably stayed at the inns where they performed. The Griffin Inn (on the site of what is now the Crown and Anchor building, Westgate Street) had one of the town's first theatres in its courtyard. Shakespeare was chief among the new breed of playwright and it is thought he visited Ipswich when he was a member of the Admiral's Men, who travelled extensively in the 1580s and 1590s.

The famous actor William Kempe stopped off at the Griffin Inn in 1600 during his jig from London to Norwich. Kempe had performed for the queen and was a player in Shakespeare's travelling troupe. The Puritans, however, disapproved of theatrical entertainment, and on one occasion the bailiffs paid the players not to perform in the town. They considered the theatre attracted 'lewd disposed persons' and that the actors were 'disturbers of the peace' and, therefore, to be discouraged.

During Elizabeth's reign more and more people moved from the countryside into the town and Ipswich was filling up. Before the Reformation much of the available land had already been built on, but afterwards the old friary sites were eagerly sought for development. Land was also required for new hospitals and poorhouses, as part of the fall out from the Reformation.

Following an increase in vagrancy, Ipswich was one of the first towns in the kingdom to levy a compulsory poor rate to finance the care of the 'indigent' who, in earlier times, would have been cared for by the now dissolved religious orders. Throughout the mediaeval period the 'impotent poor' had been a perennial problem to the town authorities, and in Elizabethan times the situation grew worse with beggars on the streets and at all the main town gates. The plague resulted in many old people having no one to look after them, the young having succumbed easily with no resistance to the disease. The indigent and dispossessed suffered visibly in what is referred to as the 'economic dislocation' of the 16th century, and in 1568 the borough decided to establish a poorhouse in the parish of St Mary Quay to complement the work of the Tooley Foundation. In May 1570 a 'pycture of the quene' was purchased (for 25 shillings), and two years later the queen granted the new foundation a charter, to be known as Christ's Hospital.

Attached to the Hospital was a workhouse for the 'vagrants and idlers' apprehended in the street by the town beadle. In 1573 one enthusiastic beadle was offered an incentive of two pence for 'everye unruly person' that he brought to the workhouse. In just three months he sent some 95 vagrants to be 'punished and cured of their indolence'.

John Webb wrote that the men and women admitted into the Tooley Foundation were normally required to be poor Ipswich inhabitants who were unable to live without help. They were given free accommodation, an allocation of fuel, and 'a livery which was renewed every other year'. Inmates were required to wear the red-and-blue badge to identify them as recipients of the Foundation's help.

To alleviate the townspeople's financial burden, parish constables were charged with seeking out those out-of-town vagrants who were hoping to settle in the town and thus be admitted to the hospital or almshouse. Newcomers had no immediate rights and were required to produce evidence that they had been born in the town or lived there for at least three years. The parish overseers spent much of their time smoking out any 'outsiders' who were likely to be a burden and attempting to remove them to their own, or another, parish.

A wealthy portman, William Smart (died 1598), was one of the last public-spirited burgesses of Ipswich, and in 1593 he helped to set up a system of poor relief in the town. From 1597 onwards, parishes were allowed to levy a poor rate, although in 1601 the Poor Law Act of that year laid the basis for a more permanent and universal solution. William Smart's bequest provided additional endowments to the town almshouses in 1599, when they became known as Tooley's and Smart Almshouses. By the time the diarist John Evelyn visited in 1677 he was able to record that 'there is not any beggar asks for alms in the whole place, a thing very extraordinary'.

During the first 30 years of the 17th century, the town quays that had for centuries been used almost exclusively for trade took on a new role as embarkation points for passengers joining the newly converted cargo vessels for passage to what are now the eastern states of America. In December 1606, three ships set sail for the New World under a charter granted by James I (reigned 1603–1625). They carried 105 settlers who would found the first permanent English-speaking colony (13 years before the Founding Fathers on the *Mayflower*).

Samuel Ward's preaching is credited with being one of the reasons for the increased emigration of Ipswich families to the New World, and his

A replica of the 17th-century *Discovery* in front of the Customs House.

Beyond the Horizon by Dan Savage (2008) on Orwell Quay commemorates 400 years since the founding of America.

brother, Nathaniel Ward, was first minister of Ipswich, Massachusetts. Prior to Nathaniel Ward's arrival in 1633 a tribe of Agawam Indians lived on the site, but Ward changed the settlement name to Ipswich because 'the settlers preferred English names to Indian names in order to be considered proper'. He drafted a code of laws for use in the new colony, and the document became the first set of laws ever to be used in the United States of America.

Planters for Virginia were recruited from Ipswich in 1620, a few years after the town had ventured £100 in the Virginia Voyage. By 1638 the number of ships crossing the Atlantic numbered around 20, carrying over 3,000 passengers, many from Ipswich.

While life might have been harsh in the colonies, those left behind were to live through the Civil War. In the early years of the conflict one or two of the town's Royalists attempted to hijack proceedings of the town's administration, but the majority determined that there would be no deviation from uncompromising support for Parliament. Historians agree that in no other shire was support for Parliament more widespread than in Suffolk, and there were few towns in England where the corporation was more thoroughly sympathetic to Parliament than in Ipswich.

The Ipswich magistrates complained to the House of Commons about 'the unhappy misunderstanding between King and Parliament' which was affecting the town badly, but in general Ipswich was remote from any fighting and, for most of the time, more or less carried on at its own pace. When the king was executed in 1649 there were many who supported the Puritan cause but did not condone regicide. The famous recorder of the borough, Nathaniel Bacon (died 1660), completed *The Annalls of Ipswiche* by writing that the last day of January 1649 (the day of the king's execution) 'putts a sad period unto my penn'.

Only in 1642, when it was rumoured that the king's army might descend on the town, did the corporation turn its attention to fortifying the ramparts. Their condition had deteriorated so badly that sections were

Troops were billeted at the White Horse inn during the Civil War. A Georgian façade hides its 16th-century timber framing.

incorporated into people's backyards. No riots or unrest took place in the town and no battles were fought there, which was just as well since the earthen defences would not have lasted long in the face of hostile troops.

In addition to work on the ramparts, 100 muskets and six barrels of gunpowder were purchased with another two barrels to follow, and in 1643 a night watch was set up from 'six to six and not one to depart before the other come'.

At various times during the war, Parliamentary troops were billeted in the town, almost exclusively at inns. The records show that there were over 30 such inns, the largest being the Golden Lion, the White Horse and the Greyhound, which took between 10 and 12 troopers each. The strain on the town coffers was considerable, and in 1653 the bailiffs wrote to the Admiralty offices that there were 900 seamen and soldiers under their care 'that continually call for meate, drinke and physicke and surgery'. They were already £1,900 in debt and were hoping for reimbursement of some £2,000 from the Commissioners. A fierce argument began, however, and the Commissioners avoided

Brass farthing token of Robert Rednall, an Ipswich tradesman, dated 1663 (David Kightley).

payment by pointing to the dire state of catering provided by the Ipswich victuallers and the daily complaints of the 'poore saylors'.

Puritan ideals were also the spur for another iconoclastic attack on the church fabric, the best-known perpetrator being William Dowsing (1596–1668) – whose visits to the Ipswich churches in 1643–44 resulted in yet more destruction of icons, crosses and monuments built up over 300 years. The 'scandalous pictures' (stained-glass windows) and other 'Popish ornaments' were to be purged as superfluous to religious practice.

At the restoration of the monarchy in 1660 the Puritan movement, which had profited from the religious freedom that prevailed during the Commonwealth, proliferated into non-conformist sects. The breakdown of the national government during the Civil War meant the collapse of censorship, and the widespread distribution of pamphlets in the 1640s and 1650s made the establishment of these sects easier. Many, especially the Quakers, put down roots in Ipswich and were later to have huge influence on the town's fortunes in the 19th century.

The population rise following the end of the Civil War put a considerable strain on town resources and fabric. When Daniel Defoe visited (in 1668) he found the town densely populated, as the numerous ship masters 'had large families who lived plentifully and in very good houses in the town, and several streets were chiefly

Obverse of the Rednall farthing with the Haberdashers' livery company arms (David Kightley).

inhabited by such'. He heard that vessels on the rivers numbered 'above one hundred sail' and that the masters of these ships all dwelt in Ipswich.

At this time there was a shortage of coins and the issue of tiny silver halfpennies failed to supply the need. As a result, shopkeepers gave customers change in the form of specially-made tokens, which could only be redeemed by the coin's owner. The tokens invariably incorporated livery arms in the inscription together with 'grocer' or other trade, and sometimes the trader's name and date of issue. Between 1648 and 1672 there were about 40 issuers of tokens in Ipswich.

The Sparrowe family were among the first to welcome the return of Charles II (reigned 1660–85). There were celebrations, too, at Christchurch Mansion, given by Leicester Devereux, 6th Viscount Hereford. He had supported Parliament during the Civil War but was nevertheless one of the peers chosen to invite the king to return to the throne. Charles II visited Ipswich in 1668 but only remained one night. The king's entourage consisted of ushers, pages, coachmen, footmen, porters and numerous others, all of whom had to be accommodated. Even after the king had left, his retinue of retainers were entertained 'to a considerable extent'. Some financial recompense found its way into the town coffers, but it was still left to the borough to pick up the charges for the horses of the king's guard.

Devereux was not the only one to give a pragmatic welcome to the restored king (who had, after all, the renewal of the town charter in his gift). Charles's first charter of confirmation came in 1665 and the second in 1684, but Lilian Redstone writes that both Charles II and James II (reigned 1685–88) 'interfered with the self-government of Ipswich in their general manipulations of borough charters'. Nonetheless, the Town Hall and the Market Cross were 'beautified' on the day the king was proclaimed and a salute fired from the Common Quay. The borough generously announced it would present the restored king with a gift of

£300. However, funds were insufficient and four townsmen were prevailed upon to come up with £250 in order to honour the promise.

It was decreed that the churches should raise the royal arms, and the one in St Margaret's Church hung for many years over the chancel arch. However, when they were taken down for removal to the tower arch another painting was found nailed to the back – of the Prince of Wales' Feathers, dated 1660. There was no Prince of Wales in 1660 so why it was commissioned remains a mystery. A similar painting is found at the Church of St Stephen, and Pevsner writes that he can offer no explanation, 'unless it applies to Monmouth'. Whether, or not, there was a secret supporter of Charles II's illegitimate son has never been discovered, but if there was he would have been a disappointed man as Monmouth's rebellion failed and he was executed.

St Margaret's also has an elaborate tribute to William III and Mary II (1689–1702), who came jointly to the throne in 1689 to replace the unpopular James II. The rafter panels bear a heraldic tribute to William and Mary inspired by the curate Cave Beck, who was not only guardian and tutor to the children of the 7th Viscount Hereford at Christchurch Mansion but also a Royalist agent in the Civil War and master of Ipswich School. The reign of William and Mary was to witness a new influence on the life of the town and inject new blood into the Ipswich mix.

CHAPTER SIX

DISSENTERS AND COFFEE SHOPS

When Celia Fiennes visited 'Ipswitch' in 1698, she found that it was 'a very clean town...their streetes of a good size well pitch'd with small stones, [and] a good Market Cross railed in'. On further enquiry, however, she found the town 'a little disregarded', things generally depressed and the people guilty of 'pride and sloth'. At a loss to understand why more was not made of an industry supplying the ships, it was obvious that the glory years of the sizeable mediaeval and Tudor merchant fleets, with the attendant chandleries, craftsmen, rope-makers, victuallers and crews had gone and a malaise set in. There was also the insurmountable problem of the River Orwell silting up and large ships no longer being able to come alongside the quays.

The influx of Huguenots during the 1690s acted as a fillip to the commercial life of the town, and it was hoped they would breath new life into the linen and woollen weaving industries. The Huguenots were Calvinistic French Protestants, engaged in conflict with the Roman Catholic majority in their homeland. Friction had existed since Louis XIV revoked the Edict of Nantes, thus removing what freedom they had to practice their faith. Many, fearing religious persecution, fled to England. James II had not liked the Huguenots and sent advisers to investigate the 'silk weaving community at Ipswich', although their economic worth stayed his further interference. William III and Mary II however, welcomed them but they were still expected to comply with naturalisation laws and integrate into the community.

White's Directory records that 'in 1693, the corporation entered into an engagement with 50 families of French Protestants, skilled in the manufacture of *lutestring,* to settle in the town, promising to support them liberally'. Lutestring was a type of silk used for ladies' dresses and ribbons and was much in demand.

They lived in St Mary Elms parish where Balthasar Gardemau, a Huguenot educated at Saumur Academy, ministered to them and taught their children. He also set a fine example of integration by marrying the widow of Sir Nicholas Bacon.

Weaving had been a standing industry in Ipswich since the 13th century, but it was only in the Tudor period that it became controlled by the borough. Lilian Redstone writes that 'ordinances for the Ipswich clothworkers were drawn up in 1590 and the clothworkers and the tailors were incorporated by charter in 1619'. The town merchants organised the making of the cloth throughout the Suffolk villages and marketed it through the Low Countries and beyond. Such was its growth that the cloth market had moved in 1447 'from the narrow quarters in St Lawrence Lane to more spacious premises above and below the Moot Hall'. Unfortunately, the markets had fallen away. In 1622 it was estimated that clothiers had lost over £30,000 as a direct result of the bankruptcy of the Ipswich merchants.

The corporation set up linen, silk and woollen weaving facilities for the Huguenot craftsmen and women but many ventures were unsuccessful. The same thing had been tried with better success under Edward III, who had introduced the Walloons – expert weavers and wool workers – to Ipswich, establishing the basis for a thriving cottage industry. But things were different now, and the town was in the doldrums. *White's* recorded that after remaining in Ipswich for some time '[the Huguenots] appear to have removed to Norwich'.

Daniel Defoe also observed that there was 'no settled manufacture' in the town and that the linen manufacturing set up for the Huguenots 'had not met with so much success as was expected'. There was, though, some spinning being done 'for other towns where manufacturers are settled', namely Norwich.

However, a visit by William III in 1693 cheered things up somewhat, with the king being entertained at a banquet, which cost £30 19s 5d. Wodderspoon recounted that a full-length picture of the king hung in the Council Chambers 'which was originally intended to represent James II, but that sovereign having abdicated while the painting was in progress, the features were changed to those of the new King – the old drapery remaining'. In former, more prosperous, times, the old portrait would have been discarded and a new one commissioned.

The character of Ipswich was changing again, but now it was, in accordance with the times, a provincial town reliant on its own resources rather than one of immediate importance in the realm. Defoe wrote that 'the neighbourhood of London, which sucks the vitals of trade in this Island to itself, is the chief reason of any decay of business in [Ipswich]'.

Whereas trade had formerly gone from Ipswich to other parts of the world, it began to centre instead on less profitable coastal traffic. Kings and queens found no reason to beat a path to visit the rich merchants, since there were none; courtiers and men of importance and wealth no longer had large houses in the town. The internationalism of the pre-Reformation pilgrim trade was long gone and the fame of the Shrine of Our Lady barely remembered. Even the great mansions were in ruin. Lilian Redstone writes that 'the great Tudor houses were let out into tenements and fell into decay. Seckford House was partly demolished in 1744...Curson House was in a ruinous condition by 1764, and the remains of Wingfield House had by then become the Tankard Inn'. Wingfield House had once formed part of the extensive mansion of Sir Anthony Wingfield, one of the executors of Henry VIII.

The earthen defences, started by the Wuffinga kings and rebuilt with enthusiasm in the reign of King John, had been the town enclosure for around 600 hundred years. Now they had fallen into disrepair and were of little use. The borough had already begun to sell off parts of the rampart to private owners, and their erosion was a symbol of the depression that fell on the town for a large part of the 18th century.

Yet there was some progress amid the doom and gloom: the 1689 Toleration Act meant that religious freedom had moved a step forward in that dissenters (other than Roman Catholics and Unitarians) were given freedom of worship. This encouraged the establishment of several non-conformist sects, whose members, in spite of the prevailing climate, industriously attempted to restore the town's reputation as a shipbuilding port.

The Huguenot businessman Claude Fonnereau bought Christchurch Mansion in 1732, thus saving it from ruin. The Fonnereau family were descended from the Earls of Ivry (hence Fonnereau and Ivry Streets) from Poitiers in Normandy. Zacharie de Valliquerville (surnamed de Fonnereau) fled from France in 1685. He settled in London and his eldest son, Claude, became a naturalised Englishman in 1693. Claude made a fortune trading as a London-Hamburg merchant and, in time-honoured fashion, decided he needed a house in the country. He bought property in Suffolk including Christchurch Mansion, after hearing that the Devereux family, who had all but died out, had put it up for sale. The Fonnereaus were to live in Christchurch until the beginning of the 20th century.

Once dissenters were free to practice their religion openly, meeting houses were required, and in 1699 a piece of land was purchased in Boat Lane (now Friars Street) by the Presbyterians for that purpose. Robert Malster points out that the founders and trustees were mostly independent traders: 'two maltsters, a linen draper, a woollen draper, a hosier, a woolcomber, a tallow chandler, a schoolmaster, an ironmonger, a chair maker and three who were described as yeomen'. In 1700 the Presbyterian Meeting House was opened for services. Defoe saw it 22 years later and remarked that it was 'as large and fine a building of that kind as most on this side of England'. The inside was 'the best finished of any I have seen, London not excepted'.

Unitarian Chapel, reflected in the Willis building.

Among the dissenters at that time were the Barnard family, shipbuilders who lived in St Clement's parish. John Barnard the Elder (*c*.1665–1717) and his wife, Mary, were among those who established a meeting place in Green Yard, in St Peter's parish, in 1686. The group later purchased a property in Tacket Street on which another new chapel was erected. Following in his father's footsteps, John Barnard the Younger (*c*.1705–84) took the business from a local yard to one building ships for the Navy. Hugh Moffat quotes estimates of 3,000 fully-grown oak trees (English oak being the Navy's preference) being required for a single 74-gun ship, so this was a considerable enterprise. During 1760 alone the shipyards needed some 320,000 tons of oak. (Eventually demand outstripped supply, which then had to be supplemented with American white pine from Canada.) Agents sourced the wood locally and bought the standing trees. Whole tree trunks were delivered to the shipyard, where they would be stored and seasoned, then sawn or carved as required 'for the myriad purposes of a ship's requirements'. Workmen plied their trades in workshops on the quaysides alongside 'sailmakers, shipsmiths and block and sparmakers'.

In 1739 the Spanish Wars necessitated a sudden demand for warships, and the Barnards, with yards at both Ipswich and Harwich, were favoured with orders that the naval dockyards were unable to fulfil. Robert Malster writes that the Barnard yards 'received a contract for the *Bideford*, the keel being laid on the St Clement's Yard on 6 November 1739'. Between 1742 and 1782 Barnard built 26 warships at Harwich and three in Ipswich, but this was not enough to keep the yards solvent. John Barnard was declared bankrupt in 1781 and his sons moved to London.

Under Queen Anne (reigned 1702–1714) the popularity of the Coffee House as a fashionable meeting place developed. The oldest and most famous in Ipswich was Dod's (later to be known as Bamford's), which stood at the corner of Tower Street and Tavern Street. It reputedly started life as a wine shop run by the forbears of Geoffrey Chaucer, who famously satirised the merchants of Ipswich in *The Canterbury Tales*. When a young Frenchman, Francois de La Rochefoucauld, visited it in 1784 he recorded that 'all gather every evening in a coffee house, where one can play cards and eat, which is very convenient for strangers'.

The coffee houses observed very precise traditions and were great social levellers, as they were open to any man of whatever status so long as he refrained from profanity, politics and all talk of love! In the days before newspapers these were public centres of communication, an entirely novel concept, where men could meet to discuss business and make commercial contacts. Apart from their role as servers of coffee, women were banned. Combining conviviality and the possibility of making a profitable business deal was a revolutionary way to conduct commerce.

La Rochefoucauld travelled to Ipswich by road and found it bumpy, to say the least, and the streets were equally uncomfortable. He

Café in Dial Lane, close to Tavern Street, where the famous Dod's Coffee House stood.

wrote: 'as England is short of stone, the towns that are paved are paved with cobbles tightly packed, which present the foot with a series of bumps, as disagreeable when you are riding in a carriage as when you are walking'.

Roads in and out of the town had always taken second place to the river as a means of transport, but during Queen Anne's reign it became necessary to better the western access from Claydon. Supplies of cheese, butter and corn all passed through the port to the hinterland and an improved road system was essential to foster trade. Once the mail coaches began in the 1780s the increased and incessant wear and tear on the roads meant there were incessant complaints as to their state.

As Ipswich approached the Georgian era it did so with a degree of renewed confidence. The town had come a long way from its Gipeswic beginnings as a small settlement on the banks of the Orwell. It had survived the Norman Conquest and, most crucially, emerged from the

Reformation almost unbloodied. There had been prosperity as well as poverty under Elizabeth, and gradually the town had formed itself into an urban conurbation of considerable account. It remained to be seen whether Ipswich could find the momentum to go forward into a society where towns were provincial centres, forced to contribute to the life of the nation from outside the capital while relying on their own resources. The crown's influence had been pushed further away, Elizabeth I being the last hands-on monarch. The time was fast approaching when political power would supersede the royal command. Power of government was, for the first time, gradually filtering down to the populace at large, and political responsibility at the local level would determine a town's future. Would Ipswich become a backwater, or was there sufficient energy for it to reinvent itself and keep pace with the changing world of the House of Hanover?

CHAPTER SEVEN

THE GEORGIANS

The Hanoverian kings were to reign from 1714 to 1837. Blenheim Road commemorates the battle of 1704 in the Seven Years War, which ensured the succession of George I (reigned 1714–1727) to the English throne. The next 100 years brought unprecedented advancement not only in science and medicine but also in the social mobility that had begun in the coffee houses and continued in a variety of public meeting places. The new concept of leisure spawned entertainment in the form of theatres, balls, concerts and race meetings along with a positive explosion in literacy and, as a result, assembly rooms and libraries. All this sociability required buildings, improved transport and victualling, but most of all a formal means of communication to inform audiences and potential clients of forthcoming events and services. By now, Ipswich had matured into a self-supporting entity and in due course the inhabitants would meet all these new challenges with their usual drive and independence of spirit.

When John Bagnall moved from London to St Mary Elms in 1720 the town acquired its first newspaper, the *Ipswich Journal,* which was to serve its readers for the next 200 years. A local newspaper provided opportunities for local advertising, which was revolutionary in terms of the emerging consumer society. Bagnall also set up a printing and engraving business and produced bills, indentures, sermons, proposals, catalogues and warrants 'as cheap as in London'. Also, 'booksellers, chapmen, hawkers, peddlers, or others' could be furnished with 'all sorts of little books, songs, large and small pictures in wood or copper, plain or coloured, by wholesale or retail'.

The national political changes wrought in the 18th century inevitably filtered down to the provinces from London, where George I had blatantly allied himself with the Tory party. It was a tale of two parts: first came the limited, male-only suffrage, devolving power at a local level; second was the infighting and corruption that accompanied it. 'Interesting times' were had on the hustings during his reign and the reigns of his successors. Whenever there was an election of any description in the town, battles were fought – literally in some cases when supporters resorted to 'fisticuffs' – between the Blues (the Tories) and the Yellows (the Whigs, or Liberals). Such conflicts invariably resulted in bureaucratic mismanagement and dishonesty, with the behaviour of politicians degenerating miserably at all levels. When, as happened in 1689, corporation members were divided between the two parties, not only were the various town charities plundered to pay the bills but also corporation properties were mortgaged and there were even accusations of embezzlement. In addition to the local elections, parliamentary elections often ended in a competition to see who could be bribed and for what price, thus earning Ipswich a reputation as a 'corrupt borough'. Between 1835 and 1842, seven Members of Parliament were ejected on grounds of corruption (and there would probably have been more, had there been proof).

Some of the portmen, whose duty it had been since 1200 to uphold the integrity and law of Ipswich, were found wanting in both honesty and application. Several were fined for neglecting their duties, or for non-attendance at meetings. What money remained in the town coffers was invariably squandered on litigation resulting from squabbles between the two main parties. Lilian Redstone wrote that 'the freedom [of Ipswich] was prized mainly for its political power and for the high prices given in return for votes'. At the Great Court in June 1755, 127 'gentlemen' of Suffolk, 35 clergymen and 8 baronets were elected burgesses on payment of £5 each.

A clique of freemen that went by the name of the Wellington Club became highly influential in deciding how many Blue voters were shipped in from outside the borough and in dictating to the corporation how it should run the town. Some years later, in 1821, the Tories proposed that the Duke of Wellington should be approached in connection with the honorary office of High Steward. At the election, however, the Duke's association with the Wellington Club meant that Sir Robert Harland, the Whig candidate, soundly beat him. Whether or not the Duke ever sanctioned the use of his name or knew of the club is debatable, but it was the only occasion when a poll of the electors was held for the office.

The Yellow and Blue division extended to all aspects of life: politics, business (there were Yellow Banks and Blue Banks), schools (Yellow Schools and Blue Schools) and even taverns and inns declared themselves Yellow or Blue. The Bear and Crown (later the Suffolk Hotel) was the leading Yellow House and the White Horse (now the Great White Horse) was Blue. Unsurprisingly, then as now, newspapers also took sides: the *Ipswich Journal* was Blue and the *Suffolk Chronicle* was Yellow.

Although the mistrust and suspicion caused by the political situation affected the town adversely, it provided several visiting writers with interesting material, especially Charles Dickens. When the artist and writer the Reverend William Gilpin visited in 1796 he dismissed Ipswich disparagingly as 'a large, incumbered, unpleasant place', though he did admire the Rotunda, the form of which 'is not unpleasing'. Gilpin was one of a number of 18th-century travellers who took advantage of the new coaching age. The public interest in 'antiquities' resulted in travel books for the discerning tourist eager to discover local history. In *The Modern Universal British Traveller* (1779), Ipswich is described as 'one of the most considerable mercantile towns in Suffolk, and so populous that it had 21 parish churches, but that number is now reduced to twelve, and the trade decreases daily'. The author lamented that although he considered the situation of the town to be both pleasant and romantic, 'trade in general [was] much on the decline'. Even worse, he thought, was that all the conveniences of the river were wasted and 'with all these advantages it is daily neglected'.

John Kirby, who surveyed the whole county during 1732–34, reported a much-reduced maritime trade having been reduced 'by shipwrecks and other misfortunes, particularly by the loss of the cloth trade, of which vast quantities were shipped off here for foreign parts'. There had been six yards 'constantly in use, where were built near 20 ships every year, and there have been seen in the winter near 200 sails of ships belonging to the town, many of them of 300 tons, and none under 80'.

However, when Daniel Defoe visited Ipswich in 1722 he had seen nothing amiss and wrote that he found it 'an airy, clean and well governed town'. It was, he thought, 'very agreeable and improving company almost of every kind'. He saw plenty in the way of provisions, 'whether flesh or fish' and thought them very cheap, 'so that a family may live cheaper here than in any town in England for its bigness, within such a small distance from London'. He went on, though, to record that there had lately been a great struggle between the two parties for the choice of the two magistrates. In the end, one from each side was chosen and Defoe hoped that 'it may be a means to allay the heats and un-neighbourly feuds which such things breed in towns so large as this'. Unfortunately, his hopes were unfounded since matters grew worse instead of better.

The virtual war between the political parties lasted until the 1835 Municipal Reform Act forced the corporation to dissolve the existing layers of Portmen and freemen and replace them with a mayor, aldermen and councillors. The old system was, by then, 635 years old and reform was sorely needed after the dishonour brought on the town by corruption and decadence over the greater part of the 18th century.

The advent of a leisured society meant that people travelled more, but at the beginning of the 18th century it was not only uncomfortable

Coachman's Court on the Old Cattle Market is a reminder of the golden age of coaching in the 18th century.

but also dangerous to do so, since highwaymen still lurked along the route. The cost of maintaining the roads had traditionally been incumbent on the parishes through which they passed, but with the increased traffic the old system was impractical. To help defray costs a system was introduced to levy tolls on road users to pay for highway maintenance.

Inevitably some of the coaches raced past the toll houses without paying, so turnpikes had to be erected as a barrier to prevent evasion. One of the earliest turnpikes in Ipswich was set up in 1711 as a means of improving the much-used western approaches, which were described as being 'very ruinous deep and full of holes'. A year later repairs were carried out on the Ipswich to Claydon road (leading to Bury St Edmunds and Newmarket) and thereafter to all the main roads. Maintenance usually consisted of drainage channels to reduce the mud and an application of stones or cinders to the surface.

Thus began the golden era of coaching. Defoe noted that one of the advantages of Ipswich was its daily service to London, opening up travel possibilities to anyone who could afford the fare. However, at 3d a mile it was expensive for ordinary people. In addition there were meals to be purchased and, on longer journeys, accommodation at inns. Although the roads gradually improved as the century progressed, it still took 10 hours to get from Ipswich to London in 1762 and the coaches themselves were a long way off being comfortable. During the 1780s repairs were constantly required for the very popular London to Lowestoft and South Town (Great Yarmouth) route, which stopped off in Ipswich, a journey made famous in Charles Dickens' novel, *David Copperfield*. The Great White Horse Inn featured famously in Dickens' *The Pickwick Papers*, and although the work was published during 1836–37 it harked back to the golden era of the coach, which by then had vanished.

Opportunities for work on the roads and as toll house keepers were added to the existing jobs servicing the coaches and passengers – inns, breweries, stables, harness makers and outfitters, not to mention the shops that were opening to sell the goods brought in from London. Gone were the days when luxury goods came via the packhorse trains and items such as ribbons and spices were available only at the various fairs and gatherings throughout the year. By the end of the century it was possible to buy materials and fabrics, and the services of boot and shoe makers, from permanent shops. Provisions could be bought from the town's first 'supermarket', the Rotunda. This was a domed, circular building built during 1794 in the southeast corner of Cornhill to replace the old 'shambles' (the ancient and ramshackle butchers' stalls) which had stood on the site since at least the 14th century. Lilian Redstone writes that the Rotunda was 'intended as a market house and for shops, but [it was] so badly ventilated that by 1812 it was pulled down to make place for a spacious corn exchange'.

In the town itself, the dangers of being abroad in the hours of darkness were such that a nightly watch was established in 1704 and anyone refusing to take his turn as watchman was fined. This was by no means the first attempt to make the streets safe at night, since as early as 1285 all walled towns (the ramparts qualified as walls) were required to provide night watchmen while the town gates were closed. There

Georgian shoppers beside the Rotunda (right) in the south-east corner of Cornhill (Colchester and Ipswich Museum Service).

were many forms of constables and watchmen over the years, including the Loyal Ipswich Volunteers (or Hussars) formed in 1794 during the wars with Revolutionary France. *White's Directory* described the corps as numbering 'about 200, and were bound, in case of invasion, to march to any part of the kingdom'.

The volume of traffic coming in and out of the town was by now such that the mediaeval entrances were too narrow. In 1781 the West Gate was demolished and in 1794 the old North Gate was removed. The problem had been apparent when, in 1736, George II passed through Ipswich on his way to London. Wodderspoon records that 'the bailiffs and corporation arrayed themselves in the costume of office, and placed themselves at the North Gate, awaiting his Majesty's arrival. The crowd, however, had gathered so densely at this point, the road being narrow, the Corporate body could not sustain their ground and retreated to the White Horse inn'.

Gradually the town was opening up its defences, literally, and welcoming in visitors and travellers just as it had done for almost 600 years, only now they arrived by coach and not on foot or horseback.

Some of the several commentators who included Ipswich in their itinerary noted a less well-known aspect, namely the town's gardens. John Kirby observed that 'most of the better houses, even in the heart of the town, have convenient gardens adjoining to them, which make some more airy and healthy, as well as more pleasant and delightful.'

The development of urban horticulture was the equivalent of the rural 'house and gardens' approach to yet another innovation of the age, landscaping. Chief among the grander gardens was Christchurch Park, in which the Viscount Hertford allowed the townspeople to walk and play bowls, but there were numerous gardens across the town. Visiting in 1784, de La Rochefoucauld thought that the abundance of gardens contributed to the impression that the town was empty, as 'one sees hardly anyone in the streets'.

One garden in particular that was remarked on by Defoe belonged to the eminent physician Dr William Beeston (1671–1731), combining the Georgian penchant for medical science with fashionable horticulture. Dr Beeston's 'physic garden' adjoined his house and contained 'a collection of rare and exotic plants such as are scarce to be equalled in England'. In

State bedroom at Christchurch Mansion with early Georgian wallpaper.

1724 Dr Beeston caused a stir in the town by championing inoculation and was subjected to vociferous protests from those who believed that, far from preventing disease, it actually caused it. For his part Dr Beeston dismissed his critics as 'bigoted high churchmen and dissenters' who were nothing more than troublemakers.

Wider travel opportunities brought other benefits in that Royal Mail were able to offer regular deliveries, and the mail coaches were among the fastest on the road. Art, music and the theatre all flourished as their accessibility widened, and artists and performers included Ipswich on their tours. Indeed, in 1741 Ipswich hosted the first public performance by actor David Garrick (1716–1779), who made his stage debut at the Playhouse in Tacket Street (then called Tankard Street). Encouraged by his success at Ipswich, Garrick returned to London and went on to become the theatre's original 'star'. He enjoyed a 30-year career as London's foremost actor and was one of the most influential and popular figures in British acting history.

Art and music were also popular. Posterity is grateful to a group of local artists for recording the landscape of both town and port from the start of the 18th century, when John Cleveley (1712–1777) began his career. Later came George Frost (1754–1821), whose images of Georgian Ipswich are an important part of the Borough Collection. Chief among the internationally-famous artists was Thomas Gainsborough (1727–1788), who lived and worked in the town. Gainsborough moved to Ipswich in 1751 and made a significant contribution to the blossoming culture of the time, supporting and attending a weekly music club in the town.

One of the reasons for the proliferation of entertainment venues was the establishment of Ipswich as a garrison town. Being situated conveniently close to continental Europe, it was an obvious place to hold troops in readiness for quick mobilisation. Many men in the town belonged to the East Suffolk Militia and stood ready during the 'fear-exciting period of the French Revolution'. The Queen's Barracks were built in St Matthew's parish in 1795 and the first regiment to occupy them were three troops of cavalry known as the Queen's Bays, as they were mounted on bay horses. The soldiers immediately lent a military feel to the town character, as cavalrymen riding through the streets became a familiar sight.

The officers patronised the theatres but also took a great interest in Ipswich Racecourse, which had opened in around 1710, with the annual race week in June. The racecourse was close to the Felixstowe and Nacton roads and until the 1770s offered little more than a few races a year for the gentry, with no stands or formal enclosures. In 1775 a gallery was built and race-goers were charged to stand in The Gentlemen's Stand. Cockfighting was also popular with cavalry officers, especially on race days, and a cockpit existed at the *Cock and Pye* inn from around 1752.

Whereas other eras had left their mark on the houses and quays, there is little Georgian architecture in the town. Although there was a cultural explosion there was no ready money available and no rich merchants or moneyed gentry to knock down the old and build the new. Only a few structures, like the barracks, appeared on the townscape. There was, though, an increase in the number of small shops and the number of inns was maintained. Regent Street (and the Regent Theatre) is a reminder of the visits of George IV (reigned 1820–30), who, as Prince Regent, came several times to review the troops. Generally, though, it was a low time in the town's fortunes.

By the beginning of the 19th century, however, the town was back on a more even keel with the military presence attracting top army and navy personnel. In 1797 the naval hero Rear Admiral Lord Nelson, purchased a house on the Woodbridge Road in which his wife and father-in-law were to live. Although he took no part in town affairs, Nelson was made a freeman in recognition of his victory at the Battle of the Nile, and in 1800 he was appointed High Steward of the Borough – the highest honour that the corporation could bestow. He retained the office until his death at Trafalgar in 1805.

Communications were as good as they had ever been, with regular mail coaches taking passengers and merchandise to and from the town. By 1778 street name plates began appearing, and in 1793 an Act was passed for 'paving, lighting, cleansing and otherwise improving the town of Ipswich and for removing encroachments, obstructions and annoyances'. The opening of the first bank in 1786 marked the beginning of modern commerce.

Also in 1778, land surveyor Joseph Pennington compiled his town map 'in which will be delineated not only the streets, lanes, public buildings and bounds of the parishes, but likewise the plan of every private building, yard and garden'. This immensely important document, when put together with the work of the local artists, affords posterity a window on late 18th-century Ipswich.

But just when it all seemed to be going better another huge challenge brought consternation to some, although bright prospects for others.

The coming of the railways was to herald a new era, and no one knew how it would affect the still comparatively self-contained town. The commercial dominance of the port was under perilous threat from the silting up of the river, reduced tidal flow no longer scouring the channel banks, and it was clear that its fortunes were not, as prophesied by Defoe, to depend on agriculture. Where would the new wealth come from to sustain the town? As it dusted itself down in preparation for Victoria's reign no one was prepared for the dawning of Ipswich's own version of the Industrial Revolution.

CHAPTER EIGHT

THE VICTORIAN ERA

In the year that Victoria (1837–1901) ascended the throne, significant changes were afoot in both the town and docklands of Ipswich. Although the town did not participate in the Industrial Revolution as such – which centred more on the northern towns where coal was more readily available – the Victorian era was embraced with entrepreneurial enthusiasm. Just as it had participated in the sea-faring prosperity of mediaeval and Tudor England, now there was to be a renaissance in manufacturing not associated with shipbuilding but rather with the new science of engineering and the older traditions of brewing. In rural Suffolk, of which Ipswich was the commercial centre, the agricultural revolution was as important as the Industrial Revolution to the north.

The first decade of the 19th century saw the town reverting to its practice of removing large swathes of its historic buildings. It was all change on Cornhill: in 1812 the Georgian Rotunda was replaced by the town's first Corn Exchange and the Tudor Market Cross went in the name of 'improvement'. The latter was so well built that it was dismantled 'with considerable difficulty'. The original Cross had been built in 1510 and was the centre for town life for over 200 years. It had been 'beautified' at the restoration of Charles II and, in 1723, a figure of Justice was added to its dome, a figure that was later renamed Flora and moved to the top of the new Corn Exchange.

The ancient Chapel of St Mildred, built by the Wuffinga kings around 700 and converted into the Moot Hall in the 14th century, was demolished and the first Town Hall built on the site in 1818. *Pigot's Directory* recorded that 'St Mildred's church, once parochial, was one of the most beautiful buildings in Ipswich' but, like many such buildings before, its beauty could not save it from progress.

Archway at the junction of Arcade Street with Elm Street, cut through a one-time bank in the 19th century.

In 1836 the first police station was opened in the Town Hall and peacekeeping in the town was entrusted to 23 parish constables and a number of night watchmen. Crime and disorder, much of it brought about by alcohol consumption, was a serious problem in the early years of the century but there was no formal training for officers, who had only the guidelines of the Watch Committee to help them. One of the few success stories of the 18th century had been the removal of Thomas Cobbold's brewery from Harwich to Ipswich in 1746, which marked the start of a brewing empire that was to bring national fame to the Cobbold (and later Tolly Cobbold) name. From another point of view, however, the proliferation of small backyard breweries had given the townspeople a taste for beer that they took to with rather too much relish.

Between 1815 and 1818 Tavern Street was widened and the Great White Horse lost much of its timbered front. The town began to expand well beyond the circle of the ramparts and the streets in the old town were reshaped, with new ones created. An archway leading to Arcade Street was cut through the junction of Elm and Lion streets to facilitate the Museum, opened in 1847. The archway epitomises the Victorian mix of the old town and the new developments: the 17th-century Swan public house on King Street contrasts with the fake Georgian buildings that line Arcade Street and what is left of the ancient yard behind the Golden Lion. Just as there had been no compunction about re-arranging the Cornhill, a sizeable block of buildings, including the Sickle and King's Head inns, were demolished to make way for the Corn Exchange (opened 1882).

What was creating the renewed wealth, with the river in a parlous state and the Georgian period leaving a distinct lack of serious trade and commerce? Just as it is speculated upon as to what Ipswich might have become if Cardinal Wolsey's College had succeeded, similar thoughts can be had as to what state the town might have sunk into had a young foundry man named Robert Ransome not moved here from Norwich in 1785. His reasons for choosing Ipswich were rooted in the religious persecution of the Society of Friends (or Quakers) from before the Civil War to the Toleration Act of 1689. Although not peculiar to Ipswich, the relative tolerance in the town for non-conformity allowed Quaker families to live and worship in comparative peace. They suffered

persecution and imprisonment for their beliefs, especially in the
aftermath of the Civil War, but were treated less harshly here than in
other places. The writer and historian G.R. Clarke wrote in 1830 that
the Friends 'are distinguished by a rigid correctness in their dealings,
and a mild simplicity in manner'. He found their clothes slightly
peculiar, also 'their determination to keep their heads covered in high
places' but, on the whole, they ranked among the most respectable
members of society.

Ransome came from a Quaker family and had connections with other
such families with names writ large in the history of Ipswich, especially
the influential banking family of Alexander (one of the 18th-century
Yellow banks). Such tolerance as had been shown to the Friends was to
pay dividends in blunting the worst aspects of the evolving industrial
society. Lilian Redstone thought it 'impossible to assess how much the
evils of the Industrial Revolution in this town were mitigated by the
philanthropy of the Quaker community, who established dwellings for
single workmen, started Ragged Schools, and set up a place of training
for domestic servants'.

Their founding principles of philanthropy and hard work found an
echo in the Victorian ethics of Christian piety, devotion to family life
and the use of wealth and status for good causes, ensuring that there
would be no 'sweat shops' in Ipswich. As well as taking paternalistic care
of their workforces, they also encouraged learning and the advancement
of science with the proceeds of their successful businesses.

When Robert Ransome arrived in Ipswich he had a capital of just
£200, most of it borrowed from the Quaker banker John Gurney (later
Barclays Bank). Perhaps Defoe's prophecy that the town's future lay in
agriculture was not so wrong after all since Ransome obtained a patent
for 'making ploughshares of cast iron'.

With an unprecedented rise in population both nationally and
regionally, there was increased pressure on agriculture to avert food

shortages on what could have been a catastrophic scale. Soldiers and sailors returning from the French wars exacerbated the existing problems of bad harvests and depressed trade, resulting in mass unemployment and great poverty. The contribution made by Ransome to the national drive for increased food production is inestimable. By 1844, *White's Directory* was reporting that the iron foundry was 'the largest agricultural implement manufactory in England'. However, important though the agricultural market was, he went on to develop products way beyond those used solely for farming. Ransome was to become a revered name in the world of engineering and mechanical innovation, from bridges to lawnmowers and from metal cladding to steam engines and railway components worldwide.

Another reason for Ransome's move to Ipswich was the proximity of the river, which gave access to London and facilitated the import of raw materials and the export of manufactured goods. However, by the 1830s the silting up of the Orwell had reached such a serious pitch that the port was in danger of extinction. No vessel drawing more than eight feet was able to reach the quays, and goods coming in had to be loaded onto 'lighters' three miles downstream.

Leaders of the business community got together and conceived an ambitious scheme to create a large basin and lock close to the town, so penning up the water at flood tide. An Act of Parliament enabled a body of commissioners to deepen the old channel and to create, by means of 'stupendous embankments', a Wet Dock of 32 acres. The new channel was to be cut on the opposite side of the river to allow for the free motion of the tidal water. The Bill for the Wet Dock received the Royal Assent on 1 July 1837, when Victoria had been queen for only 10 days. Digging began in June 1838.

The project was a massive undertaking as well as an expensive one. Investments worth £25,000 were made over to the Dock Commission with permission to borrow a further £60,000. This was not enough, and

Victorian buildings give way to modernity on the waterfront.

in 1843 the Commission had to apply for another loan of £20,000 plus a levy of an extra six pence per ton on all imported coal. The foundation stone was laid in June 1839 and, early in 1842, when the lock gates were closed for the first time at high water, Ipswich harbour became the largest Wet Dock in the kingdom.

The other big winner in this mini industrial revolution was the Cobbold Brewery, started in 1743 by Thomas Cobbold (1680–1752) and culminating in the large Cliff Brewery overlooking the Orwell. Generations of the Cobbold family were to feature widely in business, county politics and as town benefactors. They were involved not only with a highly successful and expanding brewery but, later, also bought and sold corn and coal, which both relied on river transport.

R. & W. Paul, established in 1850 by Robert Paul (1806–1864), were corn merchants and manufacturers of animal feedstuffs, as well as maltsters. Their huge silos dominated the Ipswich quaysides for over

100 years and their sailing barges were a familiar sight on the river right up to World War One and beyond, illustrating the close link between Ipswich and the wider county, where agriculture was still the primary occupation.

The quaysides were regenerated and before long the hustle and bustle was back in the port of Ipswich. Trade vessels were able to get up to the Common Quay to unload, and the popularity of steamships also increased as the novelty of pleasure river trips took off. Operators gradually replaced the wherries (small sailing craft named, it is thought, for the Wherry Quay) that for many years had taken passengers and light cargo to Harwich with no set timetable other than the ebb and flow of the tide. They operated from stages on the New Cut East, near the site of the Old Lock Gates.

In 1824 the Ipswich Steam Navigation Company was formed and the first steam vessel was the *Ipswich*, followed by the *Suffolk*. Twice weekly sailings for passengers and goods went between Ipswich and London and, unlike the sailboats, operated to a timetable.

Initially the local steamships went to Harwich and Felixstowe but later ran all-year-round trips to Clacton, the Blackwater River, Burnham-on-Crouch and Bradwell-on-Sea, with occasional journeys to Southend. By then, regular pleasure trips at weekends and Bank Holidays had become a popular way to spend leisure time earned by those employed in the new factories, breweries and docks.

The advent of the Friendly Societies in the 1850s meant that, for the first time, those with a few extra pounds could save for a 'rainy day'. Such societies as the Freehold Land Society, established in 1849, allowed the lower-middle and working classes to pool resources in order to buy plots of land for house building. The letters FLS can still be seen on name stones of buildings around the town.

The expansion of Ransome's foundry and Cobbold's brewing empire would not have been so successful had it not been for the coming of the railways, opening up Suffolk to the wider world as never before. Within a few years of the mail coaches improving ordinary people's access to travel and communications, the pace of change was accelerated. Even though roads had been improved beyond recognition from the old, rutted highways, the coaches would not be able to compete with the 'iron horse'. The turnpikes, stabling inns and the intricate infrastructure built up around both road and river travel, commercial and private, crumbled in the face of overwhelming rivalry.

Due to opposition from vested interests, the railway was late arriving in Suffolk. The Colchester-Ipswich line was opened on 11 June 1846: the day was declared a holiday and the first train greeted by 600 ladies waving 'snowy kerchiefs'. As the railways expanded, Ipswich was to become home to one of the foremost engineers of the age, Peter Bruff (1811–1900), nicknamed 'Brunel of the Eastern Counties'. Railway technology also needed huge amounts of metal

Great Eastern Railways paddle-steamer with the port in the background (Ipswich Transport Museum).

and coal, so engendering a new trade cycle that became an important component of the Ipswich economy.

Among the first to approve the new form of transport was HRH Prince Albert, who travelled up from London on 3 July 1851 in the Royal train. He went first to Shrubland Park, the seat of Sir W.F. Middleton, in an open carriage escorted by a detachment of Horse Guards. The streets were filled with 'applauding crowds, and the whole scene very animated, the weather auspicious'. He had a full diary of engagements, including attendance at various lectures at the Mechanic's Institute and addressing a meeting of the British Association for the Advancement of Science. The following day there was another round of lectures and talks relating to agriculture, science and commerce and, after lunch at the Crown and Anchor, he laid the foundation stone for the new Ipswich School building. He declared his pleasure at assisting in the advancement of learning at 'this ancient and valuable Institution'. He also visited the Museum before calling in on the Fonnereaus at Christchurch.

Once the railway reached Ipswich it was immediately obvious that the town layout would need adjusting and that the location of the proposed station would affect the way people went about their business. Passengers would no longer join the mail and passenger coaches in the town's inns – they needed access to the railway station, and in due course would be ferried there by trams and later motorised buses.

Victorian prosperity brought great rewards in terms of employment, and the general regeneration of the town and quayside was welcomed. What it also brought, for the first time, was pollution and decreasing areas of green or open spaces, as industry and house-building gobbled up both. An underclass of unskilled men and women was also created, who lived always in the shadow of the workhouse. Even those who worked in the factories lived in cramped houses that were built between the mid-1830s and 1850s and were destined to become known as 'the slums'. Frank Grace, in a recent study of the social history of the working classes of 19th-century Ipswich, has shown for the first time what it meant to live in the crowded streets of 'new' Ipswich as it burst well beyond the old Anglo-Saxon girdle marked out by the ancient ramparts. In 1800 only 25 per cent of the country's population lived in towns, but by 1881 it was 80 per cent. At the turn of the 19th century over 8,000 people lived in the slums of St Clement's district. Overlooked by the borough gaol on one side and by the foundry building of Ransome's Orwell Works on the other, it was the town's largest area of working-class housing. Frank Grace has highlighted the contemporary topics of 'poverty, crime, migration, family and neighbourhood, work, housing and public health', issues that challenged the borough for most of the 19th century.

In taking up the gauntlet of the new industrial era, Ipswich had moved with the times. As the aged Queen Victoria drew her final breath, and the old era slipped away, fresh challenges were looming in which the townspeople would be called upon to perform their patriotic duty in coping with the armed struggles of the 20th century.

CHAPTER NINE

EDWARDIANS AND TWO WORLD WARS

One of the first monuments of the Edwardian age was the Boer War Memorial, erected in honour of men from the Suffolk Regiment who died fighting in South Africa. Unveiled in September 1906, it stood near the old Post Office at the top of Princes Street. The honorary freedom of the borough had been conferred on Field Marshal the Rt Hon Earl Kitchener of Khartoum and Aspall, and in October 1909 he was elected High Steward of the Borough. Kitchener was a popular figure in Suffolk and thousands of men, women and children crowded onto Cornhill when he visited the town. He came to present Boer War medals on a platform in front of the Town Hall and was surrounded by

The War Memorial in Christchurch Park commemorates the fallen in two world wars.

Detail from the Cenotaph shows a trophy of arms, symbolising the accoutrements of war laid aside.

a sea of well-wishers eager to catch a glimpse of the national hero, many on the tops of buildings or hanging out of windows and off balconies overlooking Cornhill. In 1924 the Boer War Memorial was moved from Cornhill to Christchurch Park, transported by around 50 men who pulled it up on rollers.

In the year of Kitchener's election to High Steward a former holder of the office, Peter Robert Burrell (1810–1909), died a few weeks before his 100th birthday. Burrell, who succeeded to the Gwydyr barony in 1870, was a man loaded with civic and commercial honours and he was responsible for rebuilding Stoke Park Mansion. Burrell's contribution to Ipswich was considerable, and he was instrumental in creating Princes Street to link the railway station with the town centre. He witnessed the coronation of George IV and lived almost to the end of the reign of Edward VII, thus bridging a period of unprecedented change.

The military presence was still much in evidence at this time, with mounted soldiers riding through the streets. However, in 1902 a Cyclists' Battalion of the Volunteer Corps was raised, with bicycles adapted to carry a rifle. The new recruits were invariably young men who enjoyed the new sport of cycling. The freedom of movement gained by the cyclists, and the ease with which their vehicle could be hidden, made the bicycle more useful in possible military reconnoitres than a noisy, hungry horse.

In 1914 there were six existing battalions of the Suffolk Regiment but their ranks were swelled over the next four years by another 16. An estimated 10,000 Ipswich men joined the Colours: many were killed in action and thousands more wounded in the four-year conflict. Rolls of Honour that attest to both civil and military casualties are still to be seen in factories, schools and churches. Inside the NatWest bank on Tavern Street is a memorial plaque in tribute to 'the 2,681 members of this bank who served in The Great War...and in honoured memory of the 415 who gave their lives for their country'.

At the unveiling of the war memorial in 1924, tribute was paid that Ipswich had faced the war 'in a patriotic and public-spirited manner and all classes of citizens were inspired by a creditable desire to do their duty to the nation in the emergency which had arisen'.

Schools were requisitioned to serve as makeshift hospitals when demands on the resources of the East Suffolk and Ipswich Hospital brought it to bursting point. That hospital, and the Broadwater Hospital on Belstead Road received nearly 8,000 casualties over the course of the war.

On the night of 30 April 1915 the town received its first ever attack from the air: a German Zeppelin dropping incendiary bombs on Brooks Hall Road. Not since the Norman invasion, and before that the sustained attack by the Viking raiders, had Ipswich been attacked by a foreign enemy. Another raid was carried out the following year, killing a man close to the Old Custom House.

Manufacturers in the town turned their hand to whatever was required for the war effort and Ransomes, Sims & Jefferies (one of the many successive companies bearing the Ransome name) swiftly adapted their workshops towards, among other things, the manufacture of aeroplanes. The workforce was mainly women who had never worked outside the home and family, who made sterling and heroic efforts labouring in unfamiliar surroundings and under dangerous conditions.

Normal life was put on hold and talk was all about war and fund-raising to support the numerous appeals. Ipswich took part in the maintenance of the Suffolk Prisoners of War Fund, and in Destroyer Week (1918) £431,138 was raised.

As always, Suffolk was in the front line of defence against naval invasion and the ports of Ipswich and Harwich saw service as submarine and destroyer bases. The first of the 20 million to be killed during World War One were buried in Shotley churchyard. A German minelayer was sunk at the mouth of the Orwell on 5 August 1914, but the destroyer HMS *Amphion* then struck two of her victim's mines and sank with the loss of more than 150 lives. Four of the *Amphion's* dead and three of the Germans were interred at Shotley.

The signing of the Armistice in November 1918 was celebrated in style, and streets were decorated with flags and bunting. Guns were fired at Warren Heath.

As part of the 'the practical part' of the Ipswich War Memorial, a new wing was added to the town hospital, built on the site of the former Militia Depot. On 3 May 1924 the Rt Hon the Earl of Derby unveiled the memorial in Christchurch Park. The Mansion had become the property of the Corporation of Ipswich in 1894 after the banker and brewer Felix Thornley Cobbold (1841–1909) purchased it from a syndicate of property developers that intended to replace it with a housing estate. Cobbold presented it to the town on the condition that the surrounding park was also purchased. This ancient site had first been an Augustinian Priory, founded in the 12th century and suppressed in 1536, then acquired at the Reformation by the Withypoll family, who built Christchurch Mansion. Thereafter it was to play an important part in town history and its high-profile owners, over the years, attracted royal personages, artists and prominent politicians to Ipswich. It now houses a museum and art gallery and its collections reflect town history in all its aspects.

Once the war ended it was back to business. A new library was built in Northgate Street, close to where the mediaeval North Gate had stood and opposite the 15th-century Pykenham's Gateway. In 1918 the council began a series of house-building projects. Robert Malster writes that 'between 1921 and 1930 no fewer than 4,921 houses were built, 1,849 by the corporation and 3,072 by private enterprise'. A new housing estate was also built on the old racecourse, which ceased operation in around 1910.

In 1926 the Cavalry Barracks that had stood between St Matthew's Street and Anglesea Road since 1795 were demolished to make way for more houses in the Geneva and Cecil Road development. Throughout the 1930s old houses were pulled down everywhere to make way for more and more developments, and in 1935 the council turned its attention to the St Clement and Rope Walk slums. Thousands of old cottages were lost in road-widening schemes, and the streets themselves were constantly lifted and re-laid as tram lines came (in 1923), gas lamps were erected and dismantled, and electricity lines were laid.

By the 1930s the town had lost the final remnants of its rural aspect, and its new character was very much as it is today, primarily urban. Nevertheless, links with farming were maintained in the operation of the Cattle Market and the Corn Exchange, and a sugar beet factory was established at Sproughton. Reminders of the town's agrarian roots came in 1934 when the Royal Agricultural Society of England held its 93rd show at Ipswich on land now forming part of the Chantry Estate. The

Prince of Wales (later Edward VIII and the Duke of Windsor) attended the show, although there was no hiding the low state into which agriculture had been plunged since 1921. There was to be continuing change in the demarcation between town and country as Ipswich developed an urban proletariat and the rural hinterland plunged further into economic depression.

Political uncertainty and the progressively dire state of farming came to a head when the leader of the British Union of Fascists, Sir Oswald Mosley, arrived in Ipswich in 1938 to address a meeting of disaffected farmers at the Great White Horse. The atmosphere was tense, fuelled by the political uncertainties of the day and the uneasy aftermath of the General Strike (1926). The town authorities were afraid that with the general malaise spreading throughout Britain, Mosley's fascist message might strike home and lead to rioting. In the event there was no trouble and his Blackshirt followers did not make an appearance, but Mosley's presence in Ipswich was a warning of things to come.

In the meantime the port was changing its appearance again. The old cast-iron Stoke Bridge was replaced by a concrete structure that was better equipped to deal with the increased traffic load.

During the 1920s the docksides were as busy as ever, with warehouses full of everything from animal feed to lime kell. Children roamed freely along the quaysides to watch the barges being loaded and the cranes unloading timber from Scandinavia for the William Brown timber yards. Russell Fellowes (born in 1926), whose family lived in Robinson Street, later wrote that at night there were always hundreds of bats flying around. The streets still had gas lamps, which were lit by a man at dusk and put out early in the morning. The children had fun trying to climb up to the ladder bar of the lamp-post, but they rarely succeeded. At the bottom of Harland Street were five or six railway sidings for open and closed trucks, which were shunted around by men with horses to various parts for loading or unloading.

Leisure played an increasing part in everyday life. There were several swimming pools plus the Fore Street swimming baths, where those without a bathroom could pay to have a bath. The Broomhill Pool, an Olympic-sized lido, was opened in 1938. A rowing club flourished just below the quays and those on the 'wrong' side of the river could get a ferry to the opposite shore, where there was a bandstand. Public tennis courts were opened together with recreation grounds.

In addition to swimming, rowing, tennis and cricket, sport in general was increasingly popular and none more so than football. The Ipswich Associated Football Club was formed in 1878, and in 1905 matches were played on the Ipswich Cricket, Football and Athletics Ground on Portman Road. During World War One the army had requisitioned the ground and the pitch suffered accordingly. It took some years for the ground to be re-established and, to raise the necessary money, whippet races were organised. The team turned professional in 1936, but there were to be only three seasons before World War Two cut short activities and the club closed for the duration.

For those less enamoured with the outdoor life there was the museum to visit, concerts and theatrical performances to be attended and the new Theatre of Varieties, the Hippodrome, to be enjoyed. Here could be seen everything from grand opera to American musicals and films, and the venue proclaimed its intention to 'bring culture and enlightenment to Ipswich'. The Wingfield Room was built in Christchurch Mansion to house the panelling saved when the town house of the Wingfield family was demolished in the 1870s. Sir Anthony Wingfield, KG (c.1485–1552) was a personal friend of Henry VIII and had inherited the house from his uncle, Sir Humphrey.

In 1924 F.W. Woolworth opened a store on Carr Street, and other department stores soon followed. Shops of all descriptions lined the main streets just as they had done throughout the ages, except now there were no open gutters full of waste, no smells from the outside 'privies', and there was heat and light aplenty. The Co-operative Society had been established in the town in 1907.

In 1929 a cut was made through the ornate Victorian buildings that front onto the Cornhill to create Lloyds Avenue with traffic passing through the archway for the first time on 5 January 1930. In 1932 work began on creating a passageway from Tavern Street down to the Buttermarket and a year later The Walk was opened.

By the end of the 1930s the motorcar had made its appearance on the streets and for a few years it overlapped with the horse-drawn vehicle era. The proliferation of motor vehicles was to have an effect on the town similar to that of the arrival of the railways, namely to provide it with yet more commercial opportunities. Garages, motor and component manufacturers and petrol suppliers sprung up almost overnight. In June 1930 the Prince of Wales (later Edward VIII) flew in to tour the town, open Ipswich Airport and visit Ransomes' Orwell Works. He was welcomed enthusiastically wherever he went and endeared himself to the mayor by congratulating Ipswich 'on its far-sighted policy of having an aerodrome, which every city and town in Great Britain will surely have in the not far distant future'. Hopes that the embryonic airfield would attract European airlines to Ipswich did not materialise, and by 1939 any plans that might have developed were scrapped. When war broke out the Air Ministry requisitioned it as a dispersal station for squadrons of Bristol Blenheim medium bombers. Ten Blenheims flew from Ipswich to RAF Wattisham to be armed for the historic first British air raid on German soil on 5 September 1939. In 1943 Ipswich achieved full RAF status and became a refuelling base for squadrons of Spitfire fighters.

Ipswich had been targeted in World War One because of the large number of factories and commercial river traffic within its environs, and because it was within the limited range of the German Zeppelins. At the outbreak of World War Two, vastly improved airpower meant that

Cranes Tableau bronze by John Green (1977) in Upper Orwell Street symbolises the technical development of Crane's foundry.

nothing was more certain than Ipswich, with its vitally important component assets in both town and port, again being the target of aerial hostilities. As in days gone by, the river marked Ipswich out in the landscape, only now the gleaming water was visible to aircraft by day or night. The first bombs landed on 21 June 1940, killing three people in Dale Hall Lane. More followed, and by 1945 Ipswich had sustained 55 air raids. In May 1941 around 40 bombs were dropped on or around the Crane factories, which were important munitions suppliers.

There can be few people now who do not have an idea of what life was like during the war, thanks chiefly to contemporary newsreel film, television documentaries and Hollywood blockbusters. Eyewitness accounts testify to the constant fear, both for personal safety and for those serving in the fighting forces, but also of the resolute camaraderie of the townspeople as men and women joined the various organisations formed to meet the emergency. Air raid wardens (the Air Raid

Precautions service, later called Civil Defence), the Home Guard, firewatchers, ambulance crews, regular and auxiliary fire crews and the Ipswich Borough Police Force all pulled together where and when necessary. Fire drills were carried out constantly and the fire services called upon to perform heroic acts of bravery on practically a daily basis. Night-time firewatchers were invariably young women who worked in offices and factories by day. The Post Office formed its own battalion to provide armed guards for telephone exchanges and cable repair teams, and Ransomes had a unit whose duty was to mount an anti-sabotage guard at Orwell Works.

Women found new roles as welders and machinists; in fact no fit young man was allowed to do a job that a woman could do, including farm and forestry work. Members of the Women's Land Army (WLA) were recruited in Ipswich and often carried out rallies, parades and morale-boosting parties in the town. The WLA committees for East Suffolk (as it then was) met in the town, and in 1941 the Trefoil and Triangle Rooms were opened as a rest room and canteen for the women members of HM Forces and the WLA. Organised by the Ipswich Girl Guides and supported by the YWCA, the centre was opened by Lady Cranworth, who mentioned the Land Army in particular and the appreciative use to which she felt sure its members would put 'such a lovely meeting place'. A certain amusement was recorded when the Mayor of Ipswich suggested that a special mat should be placed outside the door for the benefit of their muddy feet! As part of the Dig for Victory campaign, the corporation allowed Chantry and Bourne parks, among others, to be ploughed and cultivated and encouraged allotment holders to 'do their bit'.

In 1940 ships from Ipswich, sailed by local men, took part in the evacuation of 335,000 Allied troops from the French beaches of Dunkirk. Five barges owned by R. & W. Paul were in the London area when the news came through that the British Expeditionary Force was surrounded and fighting its way back to the coast. The *Tollesbury*, with

Princes Street reflected in the Willis building.

Captain Lemon Webb aboard, was among those commandeered. The crew were given the option of staying ashore but Captain Webb, who was 63 and could have excused himself on grounds of age, volunteered along with his crew. He is reputed to have prevailed on the young cook, an Ipswich lad of 19, to stay behind but he insisted on going. The orders were that some of the barges were to be towed to Dunkirk and beached, most of them containing stores and ammunition. The rest were to be used for transferring the soldiers to the fleet of boats and larger ships lying out in deeper water. The shallow draught of the barges made them ideal 'bridges' between the shore and the transfer boats, and they joined what was described as 'the most fantastic armada in the world's history, an armada consisting of pleasure steamers, coasting crafts, lighters, trawlers, drifters, tugs, ships' life-boats, launches, motor and sailing barges and every conceivable type of craft, some of them fit only for river work'.

A hair-raising description of the operation was given some years later by J.O. Whitmore, who wrote an account of the contribution made by the Ipswich barges and their crews to the 'Little Ships' that saved many lives at risk to their own.

In 1942 Ipswich experienced an invasion of another kind, the men of the United States Army Air Force (USAAF). Not since its days as a garrison town in the 18th and 19th centuries had so many military uniforms been visible. In addition to the men and women of the British armed forces there were now American servicemen to be seen in the town. Between 1942 and 1945 around three million American military and auxiliary men and women passed through Britain, and in 1944 71,000 of them were in Suffolk. Since there were, according to the 1931 census, 401,000 inhabitants in Suffolk, one in seven people living in the county for most of World War Two was an American.

Although they had a high degree of self-sufficiency on their bases, what they did not have was entertainment, which meant that the bars and clubs of Ipswich were full of off-duty GIs. This brought as many problems as it did advantages and there was a less savoury aspect, too. Pubs were one of the principal arenas of Anglo-American contact and a situation where bored and tense men found release through the age-old solution of getting drunk. David Reynolds, who made a study of the American 'occupation', wrote that pubs were places 'where friction between black and white GIs often flared into open conflict, because women, drinks and local bystanders made a combustible mixture'.

The USAAF's response was to impose segregation, and while smaller towns had 'white nights' and 'black nights' passes, in Ipswich the problem was considered serious enough for the American command to designate a number of pubs as 'exclusively for coloured troops', particularly in the area around St Peter's Street, where the ARC Club for black GIs was located.

Racial tension was a new concept for most Ipswichians, and one inhabitant in particular made very public his intense distaste for it. The cartoonist Carl Giles OBE (1916–1995), known to millions simply as 'Giles', went out of his way to extend a special welcome to both black and white servicemen, and his depiction of the cigar-chomping 'Yanks' was appreciated by the servicemen and accepted in the affectionate spirit in which it was intended. Giles knew Ipswich well, having his studio in East Anglia House, overlooking Queen Street.

When the war finally ended in 1945 street parties abounded, but with many Suffolk men still held in Japanese prisoner of war camps the celebrations were restrained. However, almost every street was decked out with flags and thousands of children were pictured sitting either side of innumerable trestle tables loaded with whatever treats could be provided. When Victory in Japan finally came there were yet more street parties, this time to celebrate the real end to war.

It was to be several years before life could be considered normal again. Food was still in short supply (the WLA continued until October 1950) and it took time for everyone to readjust. War had dominated the first half of the 20th century and Ipswich had more than met the challenges. The town had matured, having been modernised firstly by the municipal reform legislation of 1835 and secondly by its designation as a County Borough in 1888, and was strengthened in adversity by two world wars.

Chapter Ten

The New Elizabethans

Post-war Ipswich was so quick to recover that when Her Majesty Queen Elizabeth II made a Royal Progress through Suffolk in 1961 there was a newly-built Civic College for her to open, which she did on 21 July. It was the first official visit of a British sovereign since Elizabeth I had brought her peripatetic court here in the 16th century. Thousands lined the decorated streets as the Queen visited the Portman Road stadium, touring the ground in an open-topped Land Rover.

During the 1960s, Ipswich was to undergo one of the greatest upheavals in its long history. It has long been accepted that the town changed when it could, because it could. If the resources were there, the movers and shakers of successive ages had made their own mark on the town, usually necessitating the demolition of old buildings. Until now this had been more or less along organic lines, with parts of the town changing while others remained the same. In 1965, under the New Towns Act, an ambitious 15-year plan was announced to expand Ipswich by 70,000 people as part of the London overspill plan. By 1951 the population had already reached 105,000, and subsequent years saw the town centre suffer from the ongoing proliferation of the motorcar. The narrow Anglo-Saxon street system was clearly inadequate. Something had to be done, and a complete rebuilding of the town and its environs appeared to be the answer.

A radical break with the town's past was suggested, but it would mean demolishing much of old Ipswich and replacing it with Greater Ipswich giving a proposed population of over 250,000 by 1983. Shankland, Cox and Associates were brought in to devise a master plan, while grandiose schemes were made regarding major expansion of the

The Salthouse Hotel (right of picture) with the Isaac Lord and St Mary at Quay Church in the distance.

port. By 1969, however, discussions were still continuing on how the scheme was to be implemented and financed. East Suffolk County Council withdrew its support in the face of opposition from the outlying rural areas and eventually the entire programme was abandoned. In the end it came down to money and the Exchequer was not prepared to finance the necessary road structure. Consultations, which lasted for seven lost years, had cost a large amount of public money and left many feeling that an opportunity had been missed. In 2001, Peter R. Odell wrote that the outcome of the process 'had discouraged investments, both public and private, so that Ipswich was, in 1969, left with a backlog of lost alternative development opportunities'.

While some viewed it as a lost opportunity, many had viewed with dismay the enforced urbanisation that would have swallowed up an area extending from Felixstowe to Woodbridge, Stowmarket, Hadleigh and East Bergholt, with the River Stour forming the southern boundary. Writing in 1995, Peter Bishop expressed the opinion that the town had

had a lucky escape and that it 'would indeed have been a different kind of place, transformed almost overnight by a handful of fallible experts and a pot of public money'. It was far from the organic growth that is the hallmark of the Ipswich character, and many heaved a sigh of relief that plans for Greater Ipswich were dead.

The spirit of Ipswich itself, though, was far from dead and development did take place, though unfortunately to the detriment of much of its architecture. Norman Scarfe lamented that 'in the 1960s Ipswich took its own character too much for granted, and let many historic buildings, [and] whole sections of its streets, make way for multi-storey "comprehensive redevelopment" schemes, and "high-rise" office blocks'.

Industry continued to thrive, led by such household names as Ransomes, Tollemache & Cobbold, cigarette manufacturers Churchmans (later Players), structural and mechanical engineers Cocksedge & Company, and clothiers Phillips and Piper, along with many other manufacturers who provided employment and impetus for the town. William Pretty & Sons, which manufactured lingerie, ladies' nightwear and 'foundation garments' and became a member of the Courtaulds

Group, had a mainly female labour force of some 600.

Cranfields mills, prominently sited on the dockside, were remodelled in 1969, making them among the country's most modern plants of their kind. All types of flour and animal feed were produced and delivered in bags and bulk across Britain.

A postbox from Arras in the Buttermarket Shopping Centre with St Stephen's Church, now the Tourist Information Centre.

In the 1970s one of the town's biggest employers was the printer, W.S. Cowell Limited, established in 1818 but still going strong with over 750 employees. Its headquarters were in the Buttermarket, with factories in Market Lane and Wharfedale Road. Modern plant and technological skills gave it the edge in colour reproduction used for publishers, manufacturers and national advertisers.

New 'white collar' or service industries arrived when the Guardian Royal Exchange Assurance Group set up in Ipswich, with assets exceeding £800 million. They occupied Suffolk House, one of the many office blocks that started to appear on the town skyline. Harvest House office block on Princes Street was built for Fisons and gained a design award from the Royal Institute of British Architects. At the same time the traditional manufacturers that had provided the Victorians with employment began to show signs of decline and were gradually replaced by a variety of smaller, miscellaneous companies that set up on the innovative industrial estates at Boss Hall, Whitehouse and Hadleigh Road.

In 1982 the iconic Orwell Bridge was opened to form the southern by-pass across the river, taking all the heavy Felixstowe Docks traffic

The Orwell Bridge is the third-longest continuous post-tensioned concrete bridge in Britain.

that previously churned its way through the town. Today it carries around 60,000 vehicles a day.

Early in the 1970s one of the most distinctive and famous modern buildings in Ipswich was built, known today as the Willis building. The renowned architect Norman Foster (now Sir Norman) designed a revolutionary new building for Willis, Faber & Dumas, whose considerable administrative headquarters were moved from London to Ipswich in 1975. The building cost £6.5 million and now dominates the Princes-Friars Street area, reflecting in its bronze glass walls the 17th-century Unitarian Meeting House. Its single design fault is thought to be the gaudy yellow and green interior, which under listing regulations cannot be changed. No one seems to have reminded the designer that yellow and green are the colours of Ipswich's football rivals, Norwich City Football Club!

Ipswich Town FC have always had a very strong following and in 1962 they won the League Championship under skipper Andy Nelson and manager Alf Ramsey. In 1978 they won the FA Cup against Arsenal and triumphed again in 1981 as winners of the UEFA Cup under manager Bobby Robson.

In 1974 Ipswich became the administrative centre for the entire county of Suffolk. The 1972 Local Government Act united East and West Suffolk with Ipswich and on 1 April 1974 they formed a single county. Change once more generated hostility and approval in almost equal measure, since the town lost its unitary County Borough authority and had a reduced percentage of the county's electorate. However, in July 2007 the government appeared to have returned Ipswich to the status of a unitary council. The *East Anglian Daily Times* reported that the argument for unitary status was that duplication would be ended within its boundaries and that 'one council for Ipswich would end confusion as the borough assumes control of schools, old folks' homes, and libraries'. Opponents claimed that a unitary Ipswich would create duplication

Giles' Family, unveiled by comedian Warren Mitchell in the presence of Johnny Speight and Carl Giles.

rather than end it and that parallel departments for the county would be established for education, social care, consumer protection and heritage.

Less than six months later the government announced a massive reorganisation of local government and threw out plans for a unitary town council because 'the financial case did not stack up'. Murmurings then began of a possible new version of the 1965 Greater Ipswich plan, and it remains to be seen what conclusions the Boundary Committee for England draws.

Silent Street with the recently restored Curson Lodge (far left).

The antiquity of Ipswich is still being discovered, analysed and set into the context of the nation's mercantile history. In 2007 the 500-year-old timber-framed Curson Lodge was renovated and converted into retail units and flats with assistance from the Borough Council and the Ipswich Building Preservation Trust. It was used in Tudor times by visitors to Sir Robert Curson, champion of Henry VIII, who was knighted in 1489 at the betrothal of Arthur, Prince of Wales, and Catherine of Aragon (later Henry VIII's queen). Sir Robert's mansion once stood on the opposite Silent Street/St Peter Street corner, and there he entertained not only Queen Catherine but also Henry VIII when he came on pilgrimage to the Shrine Chapel of Our Lady of Grace in 1522. Curson Lodge was Sir Robert's guest house and as such was in great demand among the many visitors who made their way to prosperous Tudor Ipswich. By chance, it stands on the opposite side of the road to where Thomas Wolsey lived and was formerly known as Wolsey House.

There was little development during the 1990s, but as the town enters the 21st century its shape is changing again. Nowhere is this more evident than down on the quaysides, where the once-proud symbols of the flourishing trade and commerce of the past are replaced by marinas, apartment blocks and the proposed University Campus Suffolk. Spirit Yachts took up the baton of shipbuilding in 2004 and in 2007 sailing enthusiasts gathered at Haven Marina to watch the launch of the 100ft-long *Gaia Kingstown,* the largest single-masted wooden yacht to be built in Britain since World War Two. Very low tides were needed for the 40m mast to pass under the Orwell Bridge, which it did with only inches to spare.

In 1974 the Suffolk Archaeological Unit (SAU) was formed and began a programme of research into The Origin and Development of Ipswich. It set out to discover and understand the antiquity of Ipswich, and

View over the docklands with the Orwell Bridge in the distance.

between 1974 and 1989 over 30 sites were excavated covering the main town centre. In 1975 two mediaeval priory sites, those of the Whitefriars (Carmelites) and Blackfriars (Dominicans), were investigated. The SAU – now the Suffolk County Council Archaeological Service – is assisted by the Ipswich Archaeological Trust, whose declared aim is to support the work of the county archaeologists and inform the people of Ipswich about its history.

An investment of around £150 million is earmarked for the University Campus Suffolk project over the next 10 years, and its waterfront premises should be completed in 2008 in time to welcome students in September.

Excavation work continues where and when it is possible on the dockside sites. The pace of change on the waterfront is frenetic and developers have to be persuaded to contribute to the cost of archaeology. In the Stoke hamlet area exciting discoveries have been made around the Novotel Hotel area. Soon after work began it became apparent that by the seventh century the town was already involved in sophisticated trade with Northern France and the Rhineland, which is where this story began.

Timeline

AD

60–66

The Iceni tribe, led by Queen Boudicca, make a final stand against Roman occupation.

250–400

Roman settlements at Whitton and within the borough boundary.

500–600

Anglo-Saxon evidence near the present Hadleigh Road and Stoke parish.

650

Earthen ramparts built to form town boundary.

700

St Mildred's Church built on Cornhill.

991

Ipswich ravaged by the Danes.

1016

Cnut's forces enter the Orwell and seize Gipeswic.

1066

The Norman invasion – Gipeswic ruled by Roger Bigod.

1086

Ipswich appears as 'Gepeswiz' in the *Domesday Book*.

1130

First friary founded in Gipeswic.

1200

Charter of King John.

1295

Earliest vessel known to have been built in Ipswich, a galley for Edward I.

1452

Visit of Henry VI to the Carmelite Priory.

1471

Pykenham's Gate built.

1517

Queen Catherine visits Our Lady of Grace Chapel.

1522

Henry VIII makes a pilgrimage to the Shrine Chapel.

1528

Foundation of Cardinal Wolsey's College.

1538

Suppression of the Ipswich friaries.

1550–51

Henry Tooley's will leaves money for almshouses.

1553

Queen Mary passes through Gippeswiche.

1561

Elizabeth I visits Ipswich.

1603

Town ramparts refurbished and a new gate added to the western approach.

1606

Three ships set sail for the New World with Ipswich families aboard.

1610

Speed's map of Ipswich.

1640

Plans laid for the first contested election of Members of Parliament for the borough.

1656

The diarist John Evelyn visits Ipswich and describes it as 'the sweetest, most pleasant, well-built town in England'.

1668

Visit of Charles II.

1672

Ogilby's map of Ipswich.

1700

Unitarian Meeting House built.

1720

Establishment of the *Ipswich Journal*.

1735

Claude Fonnereau purchases Christchurch Mansion.

1742

David Garrick's first stage performance.

1746

Thomas Cobbold moves his brewery from Harwich to Ipswich.

1767

First bank opened in Ipswich.

1778

Pennington's map of Ipswich.

1789

Robert Ransome established a factory in St Margaret's Ditches.

1794

Shambles replaced by the Rotunda and the North Gate demolished.

1798

Sir Horatio Nelson purchases Roundwood and is appointed High Steward in 1800.

1812

Remains of St Mildred's pulled down, the Tudor Market Cross and Georgian Rotunda removed to make way for new Corn Exchange.

1820

Duke of Wellington visits Admiral Benjamin Page.

1835

Municipal Reform Act forces the dissolution of the portmen and Ipswich is reformed with a mayor, aldermen and councillors.

1837

Ipswich Dock Act sets the stage for the construction of the Wet Dock to begin in 1839.

1846

The railway opens and town museum founded.

1849

Edward White's map.

1851

Prince Consort lays foundation stone of Grammar School.

1856

Corporation Cattle Market established on Portman Marshes.

1865

Town Hall rebuilt and reopened in January 1868.

1881

New Post Office built on Cornhill and the museum removed to High Street.

1887

Ipswich football team formed as an amateur club.

1903

Electric trams come into service, only to be superseded by trackless trams or trolley buses in the mid-1920s.

1912

First aircraft to land in Ipswich.

1914

Creation of the See of St Edmundsbury and Ipswich.

1924–25

Stoke Bridge erected.

1932–33

The Walk constructed.

1936

Wallis Simpson is granted a *decree nisi* at the Suffolk Assizes in Ipswich to enable her to marry Edward VIII (later Duke of Windsor).

1936

Ipswich Town Football Club turn professional.

1938

Ipswich Town FC elected to the Football League.

1946

Civil flying resumes at Ipswich Airport.

1959

Cobbold & Co merged with Tollemache Brewery to form Tolly Cobbold.

1960

The Ipswich Society founded.

1961

The last horse trough removed from the Princes Street/Portman Road junction.

1961–62

Ipswich Town FC win the League Championship under manager Alf Ramsey.

1963 & 1964

The Beatles perform at the Gaumont and bring the town to a standstill on both occasions.

1965

The New Towns Act launches an ambitious expansion plan.

1967

Borough Council's 14-storey Civic Centre completed.

1968

Five Iron Age gold torcs found at Belstead Hills.

1974

Ipswich becomes the county town and administrative centre for Suffolk.

1975

Willis building completed, the Corn Exchange converted into an entertainment complex, and the Ipswich Caribbean Association founded.

1977

HM the Queen visits during her Silver Jubilee Tour.

1978

Ipswich Town FC win the FA Cup under manager Bobby Robson.

1980

Ipswich Caribbean Association and International Community Centre opens on Woodbridge Road.

1981

Ipswich Town FC win the UEFA Cup under manager Bobby Robson.

1982

Orwell Bridge opens for traffic.

1986

The £30 million Tower Ramparts Shopping Centre opens.

1997

Ipswich Airport closes.

2002

Cliff Brewery stop producing beer.

2006

Borough Council's new headquarters on Russell Road opens.

2007

University Campus Suffolk opens, 16th-century Curson Lodge restored, 1960s Civic Centre sold for development.

BIBLIOGRAPHY

Medieval Suffolk, Mark Bailey, 2007.

Rags and Bones, Frank Grace, 2005.

Ipswich From the First to the Third Millennium: Papers from an Ipswich Society Symposium, Ipswich Society, 2001.

A History of Ipswich, Robert Malster, 2000.

The Early Court Rolls of the Borough of Ipswich, G.H. Martin, 1954.

Ships and Shipyards of Ipswich 1700–1970, Hugh Moffat, 2002.

The Reckoning of King Raedwald, Sam Newton, 2003.

Ipswich Through the Ages, Lilian Redstone, 1969.

Rich Relations: The American Occupation of Britain 1942–1945, David Reynolds, 1995.

The Madonna of Ipswich, Stanley Smith, 1980.

Ipswich at War: A Military History, John Smith, Neil Wylie, Robert Malster and David Kindred, 2002.

In and About Ancient Ipswich, Dr J.E. Taylor, 1888.

Ipswich Churches Ancient & Modern, Roy Tricker, 1982.

Origins of Ipswich, Keith Wade, 1981.

Poor Relief in Elizabethan Ipswich, John Webb (Editor), 1966.

Memorials of the Ancient Town of Ipswich, John Wodderspoon, 1850.

INDEX